TOKENOMICS

Mastering the Art of Token Design

By Stefan Piech

Deciding to read this book is a big first step. Chances are you will likely emerge more into the world of crypto and will continue your learning journey. I would love to stay in touch! Connect with me on LinkedIn, and let's be on this journey together

Table of Contents

Second Part - Case Studies

Third Part - Best Practices

Fourth Part - Conclusion

Foreword

Bill Qian // Cypher Capital

From its humble beginnings, the crypto ecosystem has grown to a multi-billion-dollar industry with a vast array of applications in finance, technology, and beyond. Cryptocurrencies and the blockchain technology that underlies them have transformed the way we think about money, finance, and economic systems. Within this ecosystem, tokenization has emerged as a vital concept that drives the value and growth of digital assets. Tokenomics encompasses a wide range of factors, including the economic incentives that drive user behavior, the governance structures that dictate how decisions are made within a network, and the mechanics of how tokens are created and exchanged.

As an early adopter and avid researcher of the crypto space, I am delighted to see the increased adoption and research being done on this topic. Tokenomics has the potential to transform not only the way we think about money but also the way we organize our societies and economies. By creating powerful incentives and governance structures, tokenomics can unlock new levels of innovation, collaboration, and value creation. Tokenomics has enabled the creation of new business models, such as the tokenization of assets, which allows real-world assets to be represented as digital tokens. This opens up new investment opportunities and enables fractional ownership of assets that were previously inaccessible. There are many other benefits that tokens bring. For example, tokens offer several advantages over traditional payment methods, including faster transaction times, lower fees, and increased security. In addition to that, tokens can be used to represent a user's identity on a blockchain network, enabling decentralized authentication and access control. This can be particularly useful in contexts where traditional forms of identification are unavailable or unreliable. Tokens can also be used to track and manage the supply chain of goods, providing greater transparency and traceability. By using tokens to represent goods as they move through the supply chain, it becomes easier to ensure authenticity and prevent fraud. Some tokens are used to incentivize social impact initiatives, such as donations to charities or actions that promote environmental sustainability. By rewarding users with tokens for positive actions, it becomes possible to harness the power of the blockchain for social good. In conclusion, crypto tokens have enabled a wide range of innovative use cases, from tokenized assets and gaming to supply chain management, decentralized identity, and social impact initiatives. As the blockchain industry continues to grow and evolve, it's likely that we'll see even more creative and unique use cases emerge, as developers and businesses explore the possibilities of this exciting technology.

Despite its challenges, the blockchain industry continues to grow at an exponential rate. As of September 2021, the total market capitalization of all cryptocurrencies stood at over \$2 trillion, with Bitcoin and Ethereum among the top-ranked tokens by market capitalization. In the past year, the number of unique wallet addresses holding Bitcoin has increased by 27%, indicating a growing demand for digital assets. Meanwhile, the number of blockchain-based projects utilizing tokens has surged, with over 10,000 tokens currently listed on major exchanges. These numbers are a testament to the power and potential of tokenomics. As the crypto ecosystem continues to mature and expand, we can expect to see even more innovation in this field.

In this book on crypto tokenomics, the author provides a comprehensive overview of this dynamic field. He covers everything from the basics of token design to the complex interplay between economic, social, and technical factors that shape the growth and evolution of blockchain networks. Drawing on a wealth of personal knowledge and industry insights, the author demonstrates the real-world impact of tokenomics on businesses, investors, and users in an engaging way.

As we move towards a more decentralized and digitized world, understanding the mechanics of tokenomics will become increasingly essential – after all, tokenomics determines whether a token is useful, how it should be used, and how it can grow. This book provides a valuable resource for anyone looking to gain a deeper understanding of this rapidly evolving field. I highly recommend it to anyone interested in the future of finance, technology, and economics.

Before joining Cypher Capital, Bill was the Global Head of Fundraising, Binance Labs, and M&A for Binance – the largest global crypto platform holding 55% of the global market share, with $34 trillion in transactions in 2021. Before this, Bill was the Head of Investment of Fintech/Tech for JD.COM – an Asian internet tycoon with more than $400 billion in annual e-commerce transactions. Bill has also worked with Trustbridge Partners, a leading technology-focused private equity fund with more than $15 billion in assets under management, and has deployed and managed over $20 billion across Web 1.0, Web 2.0, and Web 3.0 projects in his career. Bill sees himself as a "web-native investor", looking for phenomenal founders in the Web 3.0 industry.

Introduction

With the increased adoption of cryptocurrencies and the ensuing spill-over effects, understanding tokenomics has become of utmost importance. As such, this book will guide you through the key elements of tokenomics and help you understand design aspects and best practices that will help you confidently navigate the space of tokenomics.

The world is changing fast, and the pace of change is only accelerating, it seems. From the early days of the industrial revolution in the 1760s to the invention of the first analytical machine by Charles Babbage in the mid-1830s. From Alan Mathison Turing writing his piece "on computable numbers, with an application to the "entscheidungsproblem" all the way to the Micral N, the world's first "personal computer" in 1973.

Cryptocurrencies have gained increased importance since the early 2010s, and in the last few years, we have witnessed adoption at an extraordinary pace. The concept of a cryptographically secured chain of blocks is not new, however. It was first introduced by Stuart Haber and Wakefield Scott Stornetta in 1991. Just a few years later, in 1998, computer scientist Nick Szabo started his work on 'bit gold,' a decentralized digital currency. In the year 2000, Stefan Konst then published his theory of cryptographically secured chains. A few years after that, even more history was made. In 2008 developer(s) working under the pseudonym "Satoshi Nakamoto" released a white paper that established the foundational model for today's blockchains.

Thinking about the Internet's growth helps us understand the potential that cryptocurrencies offer and puts the crypto industry's growth in a good context. As such, now is the best time for keen users to spend some time developing a more thorough understanding of tokenomics and truly take their understanding of cryptocurrencies and token behavior to the next level.

Take a second to look up from this book and look around you. Chances are that even without being on a computer, you'll likely see a few things that the Internet has completely changed. As a matter of fact, the Internet has influenced many areas of our lives.

I write this book on a cloud server while accessing research and communicating through a browser. I keep track of my tasks and to-dos through software that is linked across all my devices. There is almost no aspect of our lives that the Internet has not touched. Well, maybe going to the sauna, but there might be a smart-home application for that, too.

The invention of computers was already remarkable in itself. The Internet topped that and changed the way we use computers completely. Countless aspects of everyday life are impacted by the Internet. It seems almost impossible to imagine a world without it. The Internet has drastically changed the world we live in and has continued to develop and brought to us many more use cases. You can think about the Internet as a perpetually expanding yet unfinished project.

Broadly speaking, when people refer to the Internet, they mean a network of computers that allows you to access information and communicate with others. As such, it is an infrastructure layer that helps us stay connected. Built on it, we have the world wide web, which consists of pages and information which can be accessed through the Internet.

We can trace back the invention of the world wide web to British scientist Tim Berners-Lee. While working for the physics laboratory CERN, Tim Berners-Lee created a system to share information through a network of computers (*the first-ever website is still online and can be accessed through http://info.cern.ch/ !!!*). Ever since then, the number of Internet users has been on a constant upward trend.

By the year 2000, after around ten years of development, almost half of the population in the US started accessing information through the Internet. One thing is remarkable when thinking about how advanced many Asian countries are regarding Internet access nowadays considering that they were technically "late to the game" - In the year 2000, more than 90% of East Asia and 99% of South Asia were still "offline". During the famous Dot-com crash, just slightly more than 5% of the world was accessing the Internet!

Looking at the general adoption of the Internet, we can see that within less than 20 years, the world has changed a lot. Even though, countries like Eritrea, Somalia, and the Central African Republic still lack behind the overall adoption rate, they are catching up. At the very bottom of the adoption list, we have North Korea, where the country's oppressive regime restricts access to the walled-off North Korean intranet Kwangmyong[1] and access to the global Internet is only granted to a very small elite.

---

[1] Kwangmyong (lit. 'Bright Light') is a North Korean "walled garden" national intranet service opened in the early 2000s. As of 2014, the Kwangmyong network was estimated to have between about 1,000 and 5,500 websites.

I and many others grew up with the Internet essentially always being there. As such, it is hard to imagine for my generation how young the Internet still is. Imagine this: Google only launched in 1998, Wikipedia in 2001, Twitter in 2006, and Airbnb in 2008. Imagining a life without the Internet is hard - we're dependent on it, and that probably will not change in the near future. In contrast, we're most likely still in the early stages of adoption, with some parts of the world still lagging behind. Shockingly it wasn't until 2017 that half of the world's population was online. The Internet has already changed the world, but the big changes that the Internet will bring still lie ahead. Its history has just begun.

We can differentiate the adoption of the Internet into two segments - technological innovation and the way users interact with it. For the Internet to advance and reach its current stage, we needed a lot of work and innovation to take place and a gradual shift in the way people operate. Together with the technological capabilities, the innovation, and those that drove it, the Internet finally took off in the early 2000s and has been growing ever since.

We started with an early iteration of the Internet that is now referred to as Web 1.0. This iteration is a read-only version of the Internet, defined by how people use the web. Wikipedia is a great example of this, providing a Web 1.0 experience for people focused on sourcing information and reading them. Websites in this version are static and focused on optimizing reading and absorbing information rather than creating and sharing them.

Figure 1: Comparison of Web 1-3

Web 1.0	Web 2.0	Web 3.0
1990 - 2005	2006 - Today	Imminent
- Read-Only - Basic Web Pages - HTML - E-Commerce	- Read-Write - Social Media - User Generated Content - Mobile Access - Monetization of Data	- Read-Write-Execute - Semantic Web - dApps - Users Monetize Their Data - Permissonless - Interoperability

Many HTML websites still function the same way: While people have the ability to visit a site and consume text, videos, or images, there is generally no way for visitors to change the data presented. Most E-Commerce websites still function exactly like this. There is some interaction from the user, but the data is set by the site creator.

This all changed with Web 2.0. The current iteration of Web 2.0 can be seen as a read-write version of the Internet where data consumption is no longer at the focus. Web 2.0 moves away from focusing on people searching and reading information. Instead, becoming a "creator" is now at the center with a focus on adding content to the Internet rather than just consuming it. People now also increasingly focused on interactions with each other with an aim to build communities around themselves.

Compared to Web 1.0, the current iteration of the Internet focuses on users. This increases the potential of the Internet by a lot. Youtube, Facebook, and Twitter are all part of this version of the Internet. Interestingly, with the increase in participation, we also see an increase in the amount of content and data available. There have been many challenges for Web 2.0 companies, too. With this comes unique challenges for Web 2.0 companies

Information and data now became commodities, and over time, transparency consistently decreased. Another issue with the growth of Web 2.0 was the change in access points and how we interacted with websites. Instead of only search engines and browsers, social media sites and mobile applications created small spaces that gave us a doorway to the web - but only to specific content.

The emergence of what we now categorize as Web 3.0 came fairly recently. More precisely, the newest iteration of the web hasn't fully arrived yet and is still in the early stages of its growth. However, a rough common understanding of what Web 3.0 is, is slowly emerging. This evolution moves from read-only and read-write to read-write-execute. This means that software could read content to perform a service or task subsequently. We're already on this path with the increase in peer-2-peer (P2P) concepts, such as blockchain.

Other signs of the new version of the web include virtual reality, open-source software, and the Internet of Things (IoT). The latter contains devices that aren't computers, which interact on a network. They could be smart home products, sensors, and security systems and allow for automation, monitoring, and remote control.

One of the biggest hopes for Web 3.0 as it's formed is that it will bring back openness and devolve control through a decentralized network. As with cryptocurrencies like Ethereum, no single entity is in control, but actions must follow protocols, be recorded, and, therefore, be transparent. Web 3.0 might also bring about improvements to the excessive data harvesting and censorship that was common in both Web 1.0 and 2.0.

There's a chance that Web 3.0 will change how we work and operate and disrupt existing business models. The impact of these changes has the potential to spread far beyond the Internet and into our daily lives.

While we might be moving towards Web 3.0, that doesn't mean that the way we used to interact with the web will become obsolete. Each version adds to existing functionality rather than replacing it completely. That means some websites will still exist as places to browse and read; others will have that option, plus the ability to interact and contribute.

On top of that, with Web 3.0, machines could also read that data and execute tasks, all while we circumvent letting our data become a commodity. When machines can better understand what is written on the web, we'll have more efficient search engines, enhanced connectivity with different objects, and fewer people seeking to control the data.

Figure 2: Comparison of Internet and Crypto Wallet Users Shows a Clear Growth Path

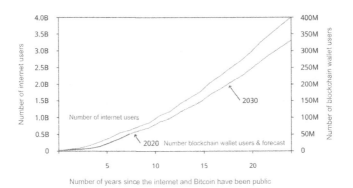

Number of years since the internet and Bitcoin have been public

Source: Deutsche Bank

In this iteration of the Internet, networks are decentralized, with blockchain technology replacing centralized intermediaries and providing the trust that enables both consumption and exchange. As a result of the rapid rise of Web 3.0 applications, smart contract-based tokens are gaining traction due to their ability to significantly disrupt Web 2.0 value pools. That being said, it is important to remember that many things are better done in a Web 2.0 rather than a Web 3.0 world.

This book is not meant to be a history lesson. Instead, this book is meant as a handbook for all interested in the space and those who might have just delved into the subject and want to understand it better. It is meant to be interesting and engaging and help you understand an essential element of cryptocurrencies - tokenomics - better. As such, we will look at many aspects, and step by step, we will dive deeper into the topic of discussion. The need for this seems clear, considering the fast and broad adoption of cryptocurrencies that rely on underlying tokens.

While individual investors are still the most prominent cryptocurrency holders as of now, we have witnessed how institutional investors are entering the space. Both hedge funds and venture capitalists are investing huge sums of money into the space as the potential of the industry seems clear to them. At this point, I expect that allocation will only go in one direction - up. More and more crypto-native funds are entering the stage, and even traditional investors consistently increase their exposure. The leading banks in the world are currently investing in multiple crypto projects. For example, Morgan Stanley began offering its wealth management clients access to Bitcoin funds in March 2021. J.P. Morgan - one of the biggest banks in the world - was the first bank to launch a BTC fund and has focused on developing digital blockchain assets since.

It has become obvious that cryptocurrencies and blockchain technology will likely see further adoption. We're just getting started. Adoption doesn't stop here, though. Even pension funds, despite their risk-averse nature, now have cryptocurrency exposure.

There is one key issue, however. The more time you spend looking at cryptocurrencies, the more complex the space seems to become - tokenomics are no exception here. Getting started with many acronyms and new concepts can be daunting.

Don't be afraid, though - once you get the hang of it, tokenomics seem less scary and might actually ignite your curiosity further. And you got me guiding you through the topic, so don't worry. After all, understanding tokenomics earlier rather than later can benefit you (and your business) considerably. Thinking back to the time when the Internet grew and saw increased adoption, those that became more active in the space early on had a huge advantage over those that entered during the second and third waves. However, that doesn't mean that people won't be able to catch up.

First Part

Tokenomics Basics

Why Tokens Matter

T he word "token" derives from the old English "tācen", meaning a sign or symbol. It is commonly used to refer to privately issued special-purpose coin-like items of insignificant intrinsic value, such as transportation tokens, laundry tokens, and arcade game tokens. Nowadays, "tokens" administered on blockchains are redefining the word to mean "blockchain-based abstractions that can be owned and that represent assets, currency, or access rights".

Many blockchain tokens serve multiple purposes globally and can be traded for each other or for other currencies on global liquid markets.

Tokenomics, simply put, describes the economics behind a blockchain-based token. This includes (but is not limited to) factors that impact a token's use case, value, emission, and distribution.

Cryptocurrencies will change how we do business, how financial transactions will take place, and how institutions operate and will organize themselves. They will impact the art industry, the cinema industry, the gaming industry, and many more. Tokenomics play a key role in all these aspects. For most projects to be successful in the long run having a well-thought-through tokenomics design is critical. Good tokenomics design can make or break a good project. Before deep-diving into tokenomics, let us first understand what a token actually is and why it matters.

Let us begin by understanding blockchains and the technology behind cryptocurrencies a bit better. Understanding the basics of blockchain technology is important because it makes cryptocurrencies (digital currencies secured by cryptography) like Bitcoin and Ethereum work and creates the foundational layer that will underlie many future projects.

The blockchain is immutable - this means it is unchangeable, making it impossible for records to be altered. It uses so-called distributed ledger technology, which keeps a digital record of transactions and data.

As a matter of fact, blockchain technology has many use cases that go beyond cryptocurrencies. Immutable means that you can trust that the ledger is always accurate. Distributed means it is protected from network attacks. When a transaction is taking place on the blockchain, information is stored in a so-called "block". For example, blocks on the Bitcoin blockchain consist of an average of 500+ bitcoin transactions.

Since we're talking about a "chain", it becomes obvious that there is some connection between blocks. The information contained in a block is linked to the information contained in a previous block, and so on, until we create a chain of transactions - the blockchain.

Figure 3: Simplified Construction of a Blockchain

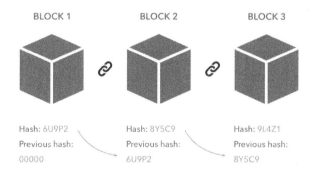

Blockchains can come in multiple forms. The main differentiation we must make is between public and private blockchains. Public blockchains are open, decentralized networks that are accessible to anyone who wants to. They are also open to anyone who wants to validate a transaction. Miners (we'll look at them later) help to validate transactions on so-called Proof-of-Work (PoW) blockchains and, in return, receive rewards for their effort. For Proof-of-Stake (PoS) blockchains, "Validators" help in the validation process. A validator is chosen randomly, based partly on how many coins they have locked up in the blockchain network, also known as "staking". The coins act as collateral, and when a participant, or node, is chosen to validate a transaction, they receive a reward.

Prior to validation, the different validators or miners must reach a consensus i.e. agree upon which transactions to include in the block and in which order. As mentioned above, different consensus mechanisms can be used for this, with Proof-of-Work and Proof-of-Stake being the two most popular choices. Bitcoin and Ethereum are both public blockchains but use different consensus mechanisms, with Ethereum being Proof-of-Stake and Bitcoin Proof-of-Work based.

In addition to the public blockchain, we also have private chains. These chains are not openly accessible and restricted to just a limited number of people. In order to use a private blockchain, you will require permission from the system administrator. Private blockchains are mostly controlled by a centralized authority. There are several reasons why you would want your blockchain to be private. Online traffic is generally low, causing the transaction speed of private blockchains to remain high and preventing malfunctions. Furthermore, private blockchains are exceedingly safe, as random users cannot be privy to your transactions. There is full transparency within a private blockchain. The users carrying out a transaction have complete access to all the information related to their deal and store it. Public databases do not allow this.

Between the two, private and public, you can also have hybrid approaches. Sometimes these are referred to as "Consortiums", which represent combined public and private blockchains that can contain both centralized and decentralized features. We can also further differentiate between a main blockchain and sidechains that run in parallel to it. There are a few reasons why you might want a sidechain - scalability, and efficiency are two of the most common.

At this point, there is a problem we have to address in a bit more detail. The so-called double-spending problem. The double-spending problem is explained with a single sentence: It is the outcome of spending some money more than once. Of course, there is a possibility that a digital currency can be spent twice, too, which would immediately turn them into useless code. As such, overcoming the double spending problem was a key milestone.

A centralized solution would easily administer each person's balance in a system. It would then permit the transaction and transfer of the money - this is how almost every bank in this world operates. However, there are a lot of downsides coming from using centralized servers - not only does the administering institution have access to all the individual's banking information. It could also easily suspend an account or simply disappear with the money. If a centralized server fails - your access will be denied.

This underlines why we need a decentralized approach to the double spending problem. Using cryptocurrencies, you don't need to depend on a third party to confirm your transactions - you don't need to have a third party at all. Instead, Bitcoin, like a number of other cryptocurrencies, uses several other elements to overcome this issue.

The Bitcoin network prevents double-spending by combining complementary security features of the blockchain network and its decentralized network of miners to verify transactions before they are added to the blockchain. The entire network needs to reach a consensus on the transaction order, confirm the latest transaction, and post them publicly.

In the Bitcoin example, the transaction that gets the maximum number of network confirmations (*typically a minimum of six*) will be included in the blockchain, while others are discarded. Furthermore, once confirmations and transactions are put on the blockchain, they are time-stamped, rendering them irreversible. Another feature of Bitcoin that makes it inherently resistant to double spending is its block time.

As always, there remains a level of vulnerability in this system. For example, an attacker controlling at least 51% of the network can commit double-spending. If an attacker could control this much computational power, they could reverse transactions and create a separate, private blockchain. This is where tokenization comes in.

Tokenization represents a form of digitalization of value. Just like the Internet-enabled free and fast circulation of digitized information, the blockchain is allowing the "almost free" and borderless flow of digitized value.

> **Example** - *You're trying to take advantage of double-spending. Your first transaction to be confirmed would be added to the blockchain as the next data block in the transaction history. Your second transaction (connected with the block in the chain that had already been added to) wouldn't fit into the chain, and the transaction would fail.*
>
> *Miners (for PoW) solve complex algorithms that require a significant amount of computing power, or "hash power." This process makes any attempt to duplicate or falsify the blockchain significantly more difficult to execute because the attacker would have to go back and re-mine every single block with the new fraudulent transaction on it.*

The blockchain made it possible to solve the double-spending problem algorithmically and introduced the concept of digital scarcity, as opposed to the digital abundance characterizing the Internet of information. In particular, digital scarcity will act as a key enabler of a new digital economy relying on assets that are liquid, divisible, borderless (*easily transportable* and *quickly transferable*), and, unlike currencies, have the potential to appreciate over time. The controlled inflationary nature of some of these assets may have deep implications in helping our society to migrate from a debt-based economy, producing significant improvements in people's lives and democratic processes.

Once tokenized, almost every kind of value can be managed as a digital asset whose unit of account is a dedicated virtual token. Such virtual tokens can be minted by any individual or organization that defines the rules governing them. These include the token features, the monetary policy, and the users' incentive system. In light of this, the tokenization process can be further described as the creation of a self-governed economic system whose rules are programmed by the token designer.

In economics, innovation proceeds and propagates by introducing a change in the context of set rules and observing how such a relatively rigid framework reacts to the change. Therefore, the outcome of the proposed innovation is assessed, at first, on a predictive basis.

Conversely, in tokenomics, innovation is put forward by designing the playground rules so that the stakeholders' behavior aligns with the goal pursued. In other words, the second paradigmatic shift moves from the passive observation of the ecosystem's reaction to a change in the functional design of the ecosystem constituent laws aimed at reaching the desired outcome.

The tokenization process, as well as the shift to tokenomics, revolves around the token.

Without neglecting the importance of the underlying infrastructure and its technical features, a deep understanding of the token nature is fundamental to effectively unleashing the disruptive potential of blockchain technology.

When tokens represent the holder's right, for example, to access a service or benefit from a discount or express a vote, within a regulated ecosystem, the token holder grants trust to the token issuer. In particular, the holder trusts that the right represented and originating from the token holds and is enforceable. Ultimately, the holder trusts the token issuer and its capability to honor the obligation associated with the right represented by the token.

When tokens represent an underlying asset, the token holder trusts that the token issuer ensures the enforceability of the right itself and, at the same time, that the underlying asset is adequately managed and holds (or increases) its value. When tokens are the reward for the block validation activity, their value is the direct representation of the level of trust towards the token holder community and its disintermediated and decentralized consensus, enabled by the underlying blockchain infrastructure. Keeping along this road, it is always possible to bring back the source of value of a token to the concept of trust. Ultimately, **it is possible to define tokens as quantifiable representations of decentralized and disintermediated trust.**

Token Supply

Key questions to keep in mind when reading this section...

- *Who currently holds the tokens?*

- *Are there limits to when / how many tokens the current holders can sell?*

- *Are there major token unlock dates to be aware of? How are the vesting periods structured?*

- *At what price did early investors get their tokens?*

- *How many of these tokens exist? How many will exist in the future? How quickly will this number change?*

W hen analyzing the supply side of the equation, we are trying to develop a view of how different supply-side dynamics are likely to affect the price movement of a given token. Questions about the current holders and their incentives as well as the pace and degree at which token supply expands should be at the forefront of our minds when going through this section.

Keeping these in mind, we will focus our analysis on three key aspects of token supply and how they affect tokenomics: allocations, vesting period, and emissions.

Allocations

What exactly are we talking about when we say allocations? Allocations refer to the distribution of tokens among the various key parties that comprise the broader ecosystem behind any cryptocurrency. Any market participant or prospective investor must closely examine allocations when looking to develop exposure to a token, as the initial allocation might be very different to how they look even just a few weeks or months after.

Allocations are conventionally split among a few key parties:

An investor in the secondary market may be wary of investing in a token with a significant portion allocated to private investors, e.g. venture capital firms, as they might expect these firms to sell their tokens and thus create massive downward price pressure at the first sign of a rally. However, the intelligent investor may cross-check the allocations with vesting periods and key token unlock dates to be more effective in their trade and avoid a downward move (more on this later).

Understanding tokenomics can be incredibly useful, and you can generate value in investments despite tokenomics that largely favor founders / private investors.

Figure 4: Key parties in the allocation process

Key Party	Details	Examples
Founder / Core Team	Often, these allocations are subject to longer lockup periods relative to other parties	BINANCE
Private Investor	Referring to any private buyers including VCs, seed investors, company partners, etc.	BINANCE LABS, a16z, animoca BRANDS, DIGITAL CURRENCY GROUP
Public Sale	Whether via ICO, IDO, IEO, public auction, etc.	ICO, IEO
Foundation	Allocated in order for the non-profit to support the token and ecosystem	ethereum foundation, CARDANO FOUNDATION, SOLANA FOUNDATION
Ecosystem / Incentives	Including ecosystem grants, airdrops, yield farming, staking - essentially funds earmarked for the community	Staking, Yield Faming
Other	Charity allocations, allocations to strategic partners, early ecosystem participants etc.	Early Adopters, BINANCE CHARITY

While different projects label their allocations in different ways, the above categorization can serve as a broad overview of the key parties involved in token allocations.

To provide some data to contextualize this aspect of tokenomics better, I will highlight the initial token allocation for a selection of L1 tokens:

Figure 5: L1s have seen Public Sales allocations down in favor of higher allocations towards Ecosystem Incentives

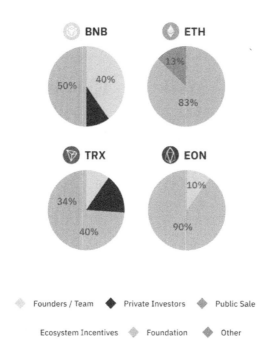

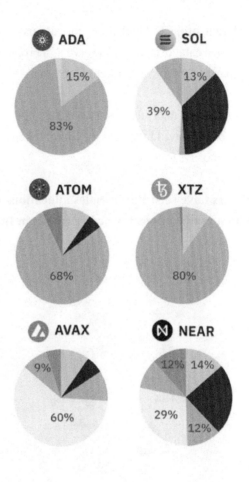

Key Takeaways

- Public Sales allocations have been trending down in the last few years, clear in the difference between the likes of BNB, ETH, and ADA, when compared with the more varied allocation of the newer L1 tokens e.g. AVAX, NEAR. It should be noted that both BNB and ADA were launched in 2017, during the ICO boom, which had very much winded down by the time AVAX and NEAR's tokens launched in 2020

- Ecosystem Incentive allocations are materially higher than in earlier years, somewhat replacing allocations towards Public Sales. The earmarking of tokens for more value-accretive purposes makes sense from a protocol perspective and can be an effective way to incentivize market participants to work on improving a product

- Allocations to Early Adopters/Developers are on the rise, coinciding with the increasing noise around community rewards, which has become more of a discussion topic in recent times following the revival that token airdrops have seen (See Airdrops section below)

While no particular allocation serves as a "one-size-fits-all" model for upcoming projects, and projects have chosen to go down very different routes, there are some basic ideas to think about when considering token design. Founders can definitely retain some optionality and do not have to follow a set route. Still, I believe there are some key questions that any crypto entrepreneur can ask themselves when deciding upon the allocation of their token.

1] Centralization Risks

- Are too many tokens concentrated among the Founders and Private Investors? Research showed a ~32% average among the selection of L1 tokens

- Which party has control if a significant amount is allocated towards Ecosystem Incentives / Foundation / Others?

2) Participation Rewards

- Do you want to reward early adopters/developers? Is this done via airdrop/direct allocations? Data showed that L1s are demonstrating increasing interest in this area, with newer chains using significant portions of tokens for early users

- What is the best balance between rewarding early usage versus keeping tokens for future incentives?

3) Foundation

- How much supply does the Foundation control? Does the Foundation have any community vote feature, or is it privately run? The selected sample had a ~11% average for Foundation allocations

- Is there a significant overlap between the core team and the Foundation's board members? The sample showed mixed results here. While some projects have strictly no overlap, others have historically been more relaxed

Vesting Periods

The vesting period refers to the time period where the sale of a token is restricted after initial distribution and is commonly also called the lockup period. The tokens are traditionally unlocked at regular intervals during a given period, with these intervals differing in length depending on which type of token holder it is, and of course, varying between projects. The vesting can be divided into two primary categories; time-based and trigger-based. While a time-based vest begins at some agreed-upon date, trigger-based vesting is typically kicked off following a token generation event, a mainnet launch, or the token's listing.

Figure 6: Trigger-based vesting is more common

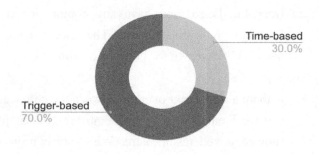

Time-based
30.0%

Trigger-based
70.0%

Source: Lauren Stephanian

Token lock-up periods are important incentivization tools to ensure that developer and insider motivations are aligned with those of token buyers. They are also used to prevent large fluctuations in price, which could come from early investors dumping near the start of a project. Further on, it can also mean that investors can plan for price fluctuations in advance of a major token unlock date. The importance of lockups and vesting must not be underestimated, and academic literature is supportive. S.T. Howell et al. (2019) found that having vesting schedules in place for top managers' holdings made token failure less likely.

Outside maintaining a baseline level of lockup and vesting, an innovative way that a project could implement further lockups is via offering higher levels of discount for longer lockups. For example, Filecoin (FIL), in both their Pre-sale and Public Sale, offered increasing discounts for investors agreeing to vesting periods from 6 months up to 3 years. Interestingly, a case study on the ICO found a notable difference in preference for vesting periods between strategic and public investors. Many public sale investors strongly preferred the lowest vesting period possible (6 months) versus strategic investors who agreed to the much longer vesting schedules. Given that this indicates that the public sale investors were more likely to be active in their trading of FIL, versus strategic investors who were in a more "buy-and-hold" mindset, we might have one factor to explain how token allocations have evolved from a focus on public allocations, to ecosystem incentive allocations.

Regarding market trends, in an analysis of 150 data points, Lauren Stephanian found that both lockup periods and cliff lengths have increased over time. This might reflect more favorable conditions for investors, who might be more swayed towards projects whose team reflects a long-term commitment mindset. The changes can also be seen as indicative of the bear market and the decreased competition from more casual generalist investors. Regulatory pressures, particularly in the United States, should also be considered, as increasing hostility can easily lead to longer cliffs and lockups for all parties.

Figure 7: Lockup period and cliff lengths have increased over time

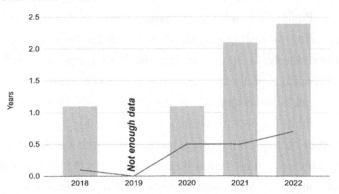

Source: Lauren Stephanian

In the broader labor market, the recent trend among companies has been to reduce vesting periods and front-load vesting much more than before. Traditionally, employees (particularly of technology companies) have been offered equity grants with four-year vesting alongside a one-year cliff. Several notable companies, such as Lyft and Stripe, recently changed their models to change this to a one-year vesting schedule, with some other companies forgoing the cliff altogether. This provides a higher degree of flexibility for both parties and eases the proverbial "golden handcuffs". However, given the change in incentives, employers might be more prone to a higher degree of turnover.

We should note that both the labor and investing market view traditional technology companies as quite different from crypto companies for a number of reasons, so the vesting schedules are not entirely comparable. We should also note the difference in the level of scale between these vesting schedules i.e. employee stock schedules reflect relatively small amounts of dilution, even in large companies, when compared to the bulkier dilutions that can result from, for example, 20% of founder tokens vesting in one year. Nonetheless, regarding industry comparisons, technology companies remain an interesting and relevant contrast and can contribute to a view of how the market may evolve.

Vesting periods remain important in both the crypto world and traditional securities markets. The crypto markets seem to be developing a preference for longer vesting periods and cliffs, a view that we share given the confidence this can build in the community. However, it should be understood that vesting periods are a balancing act, and while longer lockup periods for certain groups can be beneficial, enough tokens need to be vested to ensure operations and incentives are funded and working as they should.

Emissions

Emissions refer to the rate at which crypto tokens are released. Depending on the emission (or burn) rate and how it changes, you can work out the relative inflationary (or deflationary) pressures that the token is likely to face in the future. Emissions, burns, and other governance actions that impact supply can collectively be called the monetary policy of a token, and as you would expect, this varies widely across the market.

Figure 8: Most L1s are inflationary, and few employ burn mechanisms

Token	Supply Cap?	Emission Type	Notes
	Yes: 200M	Deflationary	Quarterly BNB Burn + gas fee burn mechanism
	No	Deflationary*	Due to EIP-1559, at times of high network activity, more Ether is burned than is issued, making it deflationary at times

Token	Supply Cap?	Emission Type	Notes
	Yes: 45B	Fixed Supply	Unlikely to implement token burns**
	No	Inflationary	-
	Yes: 720M	Fixed Supply	Transaction fees are burned
	No	Inflationary	-
	No	Inflationary	-
	No	Inflationary	Annual inflation capped between 7 - 20%
	No	Inflationary	Max annual inflation of 5.51%

Token	Supply Cap?	Emission Type	Notes
ⓝ	No	Inflationary	70% of transaction fees are burned. For NEAR to become deflationary, it would require close to 1.5B transactions per day. To date, this number has never exceeded ~1.8M. Annual Inflation around 5%
ⓐ	Yes: 10B	Fixed Supply	-

Source: Company Data

*The combination of EIP-1559, as well changes from The Merge i.e. reduced ETH issuance, should create a long-term level of deflationary pressure
** as stated by co-founder Charles Hoskinson in several interviews

Emissions are typically distributed as part of the block rewards, which are rewarded to miners or validators who are securing the chain. Some projects will also subsidize growth via inflation and issue tokens towards ecosystem incentives or strategic partners. The basic laws of supply and demand are sufficient to decipher the expected outcome of such a growth strategy.

Emissions can also result from transaction fees, which can be burned or sometimes rewarded to validators (or some combination of the two).

The burning of transaction fees is an interesting token mechanic and can effectively tie together emissions and network usage, i.e. deflationary at times of high usage and inflationary at other times. Depending on network usage, if sufficient burning takes place, it could overpower the inflationary effect of block rewards and thus cause deflationary pressure on a token. This is what BEP-95 did for BNB in the Bruno Upgrade, and EIP-155 did for Ethereum in the London Hard. When combined with regular and scheduled token burns, like BNB, for example, the overall effect can be quite significant, and the mechanic can be an important additive to token value accrual.

Figure 9: BNB's Auto-Burn, combined with BEP-95 gas fee burns, have been increasing the scarcity of BNB

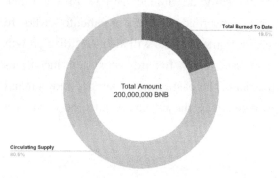

Source: bnbburn.info, As of Aug 2022

While some critics have opposed token burns, citing the asset's value as a reason to preserve it, economic principles can favor it. With increasing demand and a shrinking supply, the scarcity created and the resulting benefit to stakeholders is unquestionable.

We do not have to look far in crypto to see direct analogs; simply analyzing Bitcoin and its block-halving schedule should be evidence of the importance of maintaining scarcity and the intrinsic value it brings. In terms of the Traditional Finance (TradFi) world, share buybacks (which should be considered an analogous activity) are already surpassing the record-high numbers of 2021.

FDV vs. Market Capitalization

Closely related to emissions, and an important aspect to note, is the comparison between the Fully Diluted Valuation (FDV) of a token and its market capitalization (market cap). While market cap takes into account the current circulating supply, FDV also factors in the maximum supply a token will ever have:

FDV = maximum supply of a token x current market price

Naturally, this means that FDV is only a relevant metric when analyzing tokens that have a fixed supply e.g., Bitcoin or BNB, and is less suitable for tokens that either have no supply cap or have a fixed initial supply which could be changed depending on governance decisions.

Scrolling through CoinMarketCap, it is clear that many of the top projects have market cap and FDV at roughly similar values. Taking the example of Bitcoin, the current price (as of January 2023) is ~US$23,000, while the circulating supply is ~19.3 million. This brings our market cap to US$470 billion. How about FDV? As most of us might know already, the maximum supply of Bitcoin is very famously 21 million coins, bringing our FDV to ~US$446 billion. From an investor's point of view, the similar valuations of the market cap and FDV are a positive signal. They indicate that while some dilution is expected, the inflationary pressure is not extortionate and is known well in advance.

The issues arise when we see a large differential between market cap and FDV. As you would expect, this implies a large amount of supply to come in the future i.e. significant inflationary and selling pressure for the token. The valuation represented in the high FDV number will eventually be unlocked and it is important to understand how and when this will happen. For example, a number of prominent Solana ecosystem projects have fielded this criticism (see table).

Figure 10: Several Solana ecosystem projects have a relatively high FDV / market ratio

Chain	Project	Circ. Supply (M)	Max Supply (M)	Market Cap ($M)	FDV ($M)	FDV/ Market Cap
Ethereum	**Compound**	7	10	350	485	**1.4x**
Fantom	**Spooky Swap**	9	14	12	33	**1.5x**
Avalanche	**Trader Joe**	316	500	85	135	**1.6x**
BNB	**Venus**	12	30	68	167	**2.5x**
Avalanche	**Benqi**	2686	7200	35	95	**2.7x**
Solana	**Raydium**	129	555	93	399	**4.2x**
Solana	**Orca**	21	100	18	85	**4.7x**

Chain	Project	Circ. Supply (M)	Max Supply (M)	Market Cap ($M)	FDV ($M)	FDV/ Market Cap
Solana	**Star Atlas**	22	360	9	158	**16.7x**
Solana	**Serum**	263	10000	212	8203	**38.6x**

For an individual analyzing the tokenomics of these projects, it is crucial to understand the emission schedule. What does the scheduled release look like for the remaining coins? Will circulation double quickly, or is it a longer-term schedule? How much dilution is expected and how quickly?

Of course, having a large amount of supply yet to come to market does not entirely ruin a project. It is possible that, depending on token utility, the extra supply gets absorbed into the market, and valuations are not affected as harshly as forecast. Hopefully, this helps highlight the fact that tokenomics is not something to be looked at in isolation, but rather as part of a more holistic analysis of a project.

DeFi APRs

Since the Decentralized Finance (DeFi) Summer of 2020, the sub-sector has been known for its extremely lucrative investing strategies. Many strategies, including optimizing staking rewards, participating in lending pools, and providing liquidity for exchange fee rewards, traditionally offer relatively reasonable interest rates.

On the other side of the spectrum, users can generate more bountiful yields by providing liquidity to DeFi incentivized liquidity pools or DeFi yield farms. These strategies involve users providing liquidity to pools (often for new or recently-launched tokens) and, in turn, being rewarded with additional tokens, generally with high APRs. Some protocols utilize initially high emission rates that gradually slow down to attract and build up a solid initial user base.

PancakeSwap is a notable example of this. While the protocol had taken criticism regarding emissions in its earlier days, it has since introduced many deflationary mechanics into the token.

Unfortunately, other protocols may not be so sensible and do not ever taper their emissions until, eventually, the inflationary growth becomes too much to sustain and a virtuous downward cycle erupts (e.g. Iron Finance). This is something to note when looking into the tokenomics of any protocol offering APRs that seem too high.

As always, if it looks too good to be true, it probably is!

Figure 11: PancakeSwap tokenomics mechanisms

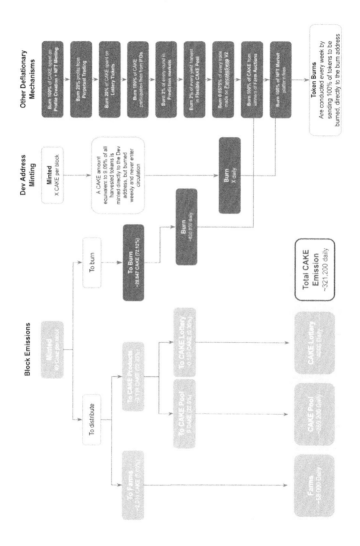

Source: PancakeSwap

Airdrops

Airdrops have gone through a revival since 2021 after a notable drop in popularity since their early peak in 2018. Rather than go through a tedious description of the origins of the distribution method and the earlier iterations, it will be more beneficial to explore a few of the more interesting distribution strategies companies have used to allocate their airdrops. One of the issues this method has faced is users trying to "game" the system and farm the airdrops. Suppose these so-called Sybil attackers are able to gain a disproportionate share of the token allocation. In that case, it can be quite damaging to a protocol, especially if governance issues are involved - or simply due to the potential for price dumps. To combat these issues, we have seen an increasing focus from protocols to identify these actors and take action.

A few notable examples:

Hop Protocol

- Cross-chain bridge, Hop Protocol, was particularly focused on combating Sybil attackers from their token

- After cutting eligible addresses by nearly 25% using their own bots, they announced a two-week period to accept community reports of Sybil addresses that have slipped through the cracks. Members would be rewarded with 25% of the tokens saved (1-year lock-up). This initiative generated a significant response and recovered nearly 1 million tokens in just the first week

- In what was dubbed a "first" for airdrops, the Hop team went as far as to invite Sybil attackers to self-report, again, offering 25% of the recovered tokens as a reward

Optimism

- Leading Ethereum Layer-2 solution, Optimism, announced their OP token in late April and confirmed that 19% of the total supply would be distributed via a number of airdrops

- After initially identifying ~250k wallets as eligible for Airdrop #1 following screening for potential "airdrop farmers", they went on to later recover and redistribute tokens from an additional 17,000 wallets of later flagged Sybil attackers

- Some of these were identified by Optimism community members, while others were flagged for "suspicious" L1 and/or L2 activity

Lockdrop

- Lockdrops are a close relative of the traditional airdrop and can function as an effective alternative, choosing to focus on the future of a protocol, rather than past engagement (which is often what airdrop criteria are based upon)

- Lockdrops require commitment from the user to receive the tokens. For example, users could be asked to lock up BNB for some time and then receive the protocol's new tokens as a reward. Often, the longer the user locks up the BNB, the larger their token allocation for the new token

- You can also further commit the lock-dropped tokens to a liquidity pool to receive additional rewards and help with token price discovery

- In comparing the two distribution methods, lockdrops might be more suitable for building an engaged community, while airdrops might be able to cast a significantly wider net in terms of protocol marketing and brand awareness

Stefan Piech

Token Demand

Key questions to keep in mind when reading this section...

- *What is the purpose/utility of the token?*

- *What are the key drivers of demand for the token?*

- *Are there protocol revenues that get distributed to the token holders?*

- *Do the tokens secure the project?*

T okenomics does not end at Token supply. As a matter of fact, Token demand is equally if not more important. After all, even a good supply design can't help if there is no demand for a token.

That being said, supply design characteristics can definitely impact the demand side, and a bad tokenomics design could make or break a project's reputation in the market. At the same time, good token design can increase incentives and drive demand. To understand why we should look at the following two scenarios:

1. You're designing your tokenomics but not paying attention to the number of tokens in circulation. Consequently, the price for one token is extremely high - and despite a reasonable valuation, it might scare retail investors away. At the same time, having an extremely high token supply drives the price of each token into the cents could signal that the project is trying to scam retail users because reaching the value of 1 USD or even 1 cent is hard, if not impossible, to achieve. Finding the right middle ground is important.

   At the same time, having too little or too high allocation to founders or developers can have equally negative consequences, with investors not wanting to allocate to the project and developers not wanting to build or the community seeing it as a get-rich-quick scheme for venture capital firms and thus holding back from participating in a project.

2. Now, imagine you are designing your project tokenomics, but this time you are paying attention to it. You can create an allocation design that incentives investors and developers but doesn't scare away users, ultimately leading to higher prices. You can allocate some tokens to "growth initiatives" such as airdrops and gain not only visibility but also new users. At the same time, by choosing the right amount of outstanding supply and total supply according to the expected market size, you can create tokenomics that will attract more users and lead to healthy long-term growth.

Ultimately, many projects underestimate the demand side by paying too little attention to the incentive functions tokens can play and the psychological element that can drive sustainable growth. Simply put, the incentive function is a key driver of demand and, thus, an important backbone for every possible kind of project. The incentive function is often tied to a form of utility that a token offers, and as such, we should have a closer look at the utility of tokens first. The definition of utility in terms of token demand is wide-ranging, reaching from governance to the creation of stand-alone ecosystems. These different utilities often drive long-term holders to acquire specific tokens. Ultimately, you must decide which utility you want to assign to elements such as governance vs. revenue accruals, etc.

We will deep-dive into the tokenomics of different projects in a later part of this book which will help you to understand the utility of tokens better.

After all, as a project owner, you need to create the desire for users to hold your tokens. The best way to do so is by giving tokens a form of utility. In contrast, as a user or investor in the tokens you want to clearly understand what value holding the token brings to you.

Aspects like interest alignment add an additional layer of value to projects, and we will explore this concept further in this chapter as well. However, let us not forget that without a good product, even an excellent token design and utility are of little long-lasting value. As such, while this book solely focuses on tokenomics, I encourage you to also think about the value proposition that the product brings in and of itself. Tokenomics should offer another layer of functionality and utility that can drive further demand. Tokenomics shouldn't be the sole driver of demand.

Utility

When considering the demand side, the concept of utility might be the most important element. After all, utility is what gives tokens a use case that is appreciated by the broadest audience. Having a high demand for a project simply means many people want to hold the project token. The reasons for this are often the same - accessing a protocol, participating in governance, or exchanging value in a decentralized environment. As such, utility is the key driver of token demand by offering solutions to problems and value-add to users. Suppose the token provides greater utility and thus generates greater demand from users. If the token demand increases at a greater rate than the token supply, we should have price appreciation - Economics 101! To understand this further, let us explore six key elements of utility that we should all be aware of.

1) Right

Tokens can allow for many kinds of different rights. They can offer the right to engage with a protocol, game, or project. In addition, they can provide users with rights such as participation in governance (e.g. in the form of voting), the right to contribute (as a key member or user), and many more. Governance is by far one of the most common rights, allowing users to propose changes and vote on the directionality of a project.

But it's not the only one. Rights can also come in the form of access to a protocol and allow for product usage or even offer the right to ownership. While the concept is very broad, it is also straightforward. Almost every form of right you can have in the offline and web2 world can most likely also be given to you in the form of tokens. Accessing a club or owning a house could be designed in the form of an NFT, with ownership granting you the right to that cool new club or fancy new home.

2) Value Exchange

The usage of tokens that create the foundation of games, the metaverse, and DAOs can lead to the creation of completely new "micro"-economies. These "micro"-economies exist outside the normal financial system that we know and are not controlled by the US dollar or any other currency but simply by the token (or a combination of multiple tokens) alone. In these "micro"-economies, tokens can facilitate the creation and existence of economies by allowing users to buy and sell items, interact with each other, and by rewarding work (and commitment). One key function is the ability to exchange value.

3) Toll

A third element that can give tokens a unique form of utility is the element of a "toll". The toll that we all know is a charge payable for permission to use a particular bridge or road. The toll that I am referring to in this context is very similar. Introducing tokens leads to investors, users, developers, and other stakeholders having skin in the game. Often, security deposits or usage fees can help to create a barrier to entry when running a smart contract platform, protocol, or game, giving unique utility to those that hold the tokens compared to those that don't.

4) Function

Another form of token utility can come in the form of unique functionality that is often only available with the usage of tokens. Tokens can enrich the user experience by allowing them to join a network of like-minded people, participate in a game, and much more. But functionality doesn't end here. Otherwise, it is no different than a key to a clubhouse. Tokens can incentivize participation in unique ways, and their smart-contract-based nature allows for unique characteristics that can take the often-flawed human element out of the decision-making process.

5) Currency

Regardless of its form, all currency has the same basic goals. Even those who are little versed in Monetary Economics understand that, fundamentally, money must act as a unit of account, a store of value, and a medium of exchange. The utility of tokens as currency is quite similar in the crypto space. Be it with a crypto-native game or a decentralized financial protocol - having a token as an underlying "currency" can help to achieve the above functions. This, in return, can bring new functionalities to games and protocols.

Of course, tokens have various categories, including stablecoins (which again can be categorized into multiple sub-categories) that are directly tied to fiat currencies.

Bitcoin was created with the goal of becoming a true non-fiat decentralized currency. To be called a currency, in a traditional way of understanding, it must fulfill the three criteria; unit of account, store of value, and medium of exchange, which critics often cite as why Bitcoin is not a "*real*" currency.

We also have in-game currencies, which help commerce within the confines of a game, an example being Smooth Love Potions (SLP) in Axie Infinity. In addition, there is constant discussion among other communities where there is no commonly agreed answer. Ether has been one of these tokens, where given its usage, it is seen as currency (medium of exchange) by some, whereas others see it more of a commodity akin to Bitcoin. All in all, the currency as a utility remains one of the more dynamic and diverse paths you can take, with many different examples as illustrated here.

6) Earnings

The last noteworthy aspect of utility is that of "Earnings". Protocols share their earnings through token incentives and distribute benefits to many different types of participants of a protocol. This can help to foster the growth and development of an ecosystem. More importantly, however, having an equitable redistribution of the resulting increased value is part of what blockchain-based models can achieve. The utility aspect here is quite clear - by offering earnings sharing through a token system, users are encouraged to participate in the projects they believe in.

Combining the six elements, we can summarize token utility in the following table.

Figure 12: Elements of token utility and their purpose

Role	Purpose	Features
Right	Engagement	Product usage, Governance, Voting, Contribution, Product Access, Ownership
Value Exchange	Economy Creation	Working rewards, Buying, Selling, Spending, Active/Passive Work, Creating a Product
Toll	Skin in the Game	Running Smart Contracts, Security Deposit, Usage Fees
Function	Enriching Experience	Joining a Network, Connecting with Users, Incentive for Users
Currency	Frictionless Transaction	Unit of Account, Medium of Exchange, Store of Value
Earnings	Distributing Benefits	Profit Sharing, Benefit Sharing, Inflation Benefits

Source: William Mougayar

As you can see, tokens can offer multiple noteworthy benefits and thus bring different types of utility to their underlying protocols. But utility is not the only aspect that drives token demand. Utility is only worth something if you trust the people behind the project, believe in the product's sustainability, and the token's use case. Consequently, creating and maintaining trust is essential.

Tokenization represents a form of digitalization of value.

Just like the Internet-enabled free and fast circulation of digitized information, the blockchain allows the free and borderless flow of digitized value. Making sure that this is happening in a trusted environment is important, which is why we should explore the element of trust in more detail at this point.

Trust

Broadly speaking, almost every kind of value can be managed through a dedicated virtual token. Knowing that behind most tokens is a team of founders, developers and early adopters often raise the question of allocation. High allocation to the founders of a project usually leads to lower trust and could negatively impact a project. Similar issues exist if the founders stay anonymous, considering the history of rug-pulls and honeypot scams.

Creating trust is extremely important to create long-lasting and sustainable growth and usage.

Trust plays an essential role in the utility of tokens. When tokens represent the right to access a service or participate in a vote within a regulated ecosystem, the token holder grants trust to the token issuer. Additionally, in the case of tokens representing a right, trust lies within the enforceability of this right. Following this line of thinking, it is almost always possible to bring back the source of value of a token to the concept of trust.

Ultimately, it is even possible to define tokens as quantifiable representations of decentralized and disintermediated trust.

To understand the concept of trust better, think back to when Terraform Labs' Stablecoin UST first de-pegged. While the initial de-pegging of an algorithmic stablecoin was nothing "*new*" to the broader market, the loss of trust in the management team and loss of trust that the Terraform Labs team will deploy enough reserves (and additional capital) led to further acceleration of withdrawals. It caused further de-pegging even once the team deployed capital.

The slow reaction speed and lack of communication led to a complete loss of trust. We all know too well what happened afterward, and even at the time of writing this book, Terraform Labs' UST stablecoin is trading at just a few cents. Once gone - trust is rarely fully restored.

We can observe similar characteristics during other events. Be it during times when the founding team received a high token allocation or when investors make up the top holders of a token. We see it when the token team is anonymous and suspiciously moving funds or the supply economics sound too good to be true. In all these cases, the outcome is often the same - the permanent loss of trust, deeming a token worthless.

Projects such as Wonderland's TIME promised sky-high return and their interpretation of (3,3), a reference of the game's theoretical best-case payoff (a win-win), led to the project turning into a (-99,-99) losing most of its value in the course of its young history. Wonderland's TIME big wake-up call was when trust in the project was destroyed after leaks revealed the criminal background of the project's CFO.

SushiSwap saw a similar decrease in its token value after people lost trust in the management following internal disputes. Many other protocols have similarly lost trust temporarily or sometimes even permanently after being "*rekt*". As mentioned earlier - while trust takes a long time to build - it is destroyed in mere moments and almost never fully recovers.

Interest Alignment

A key aspect to consider when looking at the demand side of Tokenomics is that of interest alignment. "Alignment of interest" is an arrangement in which all parties involved stand to benefit from one particular outcome. In our case, this outcome is an increase in token price due to higher demand.

We can thus see interest alignment as a way to foster increased demand for a project. This, combined with the right token allocation and distribution, can encourage participation and growth. Revenue sharing and a vote escrow model are two approaches to consider in creating interest alignment.

Figure 13: Revenue sharing classification

Revenue Sharing	Where	How
	On Chain	Token rewards
	Off Chain	Buy-and-Burn

Revenue sharing, as the name suggests, refers to a token owner having the right to a portion of revenues or fees generated by a project. Revenue sharing can take place on- and off-chain. On-chain, when a network performs an action, a small fee is extracted and distributed to token holders.

In addition to that, revenues can be distributed in several ways. Revenues can be distributed on-chain periodically through token rewards or through a buy-and-burn mechanism in which fees generated are used to remove tokens from the circulating supply, thus increasing the value of the outstanding tokens.

Importantly, when discussing interest alignment, I mean the alignment of protocols with their users, not the alignment between protocols, VCs, and other investors. After all, while important in the early stages, they're not the ones that bring sustainable growth – users are.

Not every project uses a form of interest alignment, and some noteworthy projects are quite successful without it. Uniswap is an example of a protocol with no revenue sharing. Instead, all the trading fees accrue toward the liquidity providers. UNI token holders do not receive revenues. Instead, the token's main value comes through the ability to participate in the project's governance.

SushiSwap - another decentralized exchange and Uniswap competitor - is an example of a protocol that participates in revenue sharing. Liquidity providers (LP), token holders, traders, and the DAO are the parties considered. There is no set distribution structure regarding how to divide the percentage each group should receive. Different projects have different approaches to this. Of course, redirecting a bigger share of the revenue towards one of the parties has a negative impact on some of the other parties involved in the protocol.

Figure 14: DEX Fee distribution - Showing the different approaches being used by Decentralized Exchanges

DEX	% fees to LP	% fees to token holder	% fees to DAO
Uniswap	100%	-	-
SushiSwap	83.3%	16.7%	-
PancakeSwap	68%	20%	12%
Curve	50%	50%	-
Balancer	50%	37.5%	12.5%
dYdX	-	-	100%

An important aspect of interest alignment within the crypto space is that revenue share tokens reward investors instantly. The payments to those who financed the business are mandated by the smart contract, which is itself immutably recorded on the blockchain.

Stefan Piech

Token Governance

Key questions to keep in mind when reading this section…

- *How concentrated are governance votes?*

- *Will your vote make a difference?*

- *What are the minimum token requirements to submit and escalate a governance proposal?*

- *Can governance enable or affect profit distribution?*

- *Are there bribes for governance voting that you can earn from?*

G overnance plays an important role when it comes to tokenomics. While transparent and healthy governance can offer a lot of utility and drive the demand for a token, there are also a lot of other aspects to consider here. Considering the complexity of this topic and the importance of token governance, a chapter is dedicated to this topic in a later part of this book.

Token governance allows for development, growth, and community engagement through so-called decentralized autonomous organizations (DAOs). There is value in having a native token for your project that can be used to govern the protocol. This can help to separate the governance and other aspects of a protocol and offer security to the community. For example, if a bad actor wants to vote on something that is destroying the value for the project, he would consequently destroy his own wealth in the process.

The originating idea of decentralized autonomous organizations envisioned a future in which it is not management and governments that dictate the future of projects but instead the community that can operate without the limitations of traditional organizational structure.

DAOs as well as traditional organizations and entities operate quite differently. There is no board, there are no managers and members can even be pseudonymous.

While the aim of decentralization and independence was floating around the crypto space for quite some time, it wasn't until 2016 that one of the first decentralized autonomous organizations was built. Fittingly, they called it "The DAO," also known as Genesis DAO. Built on the Ethereum blockchain as an open-source project by the Slock.it team, "The DAO" became an immediate success. During its creation period, the project managed to gather around 12.7 million Ether (worth approximately 150 million USD at the time, though about 13 billion during the time of writing this report and more than 62 billion during Ethereum's all-time high, representing nearly 14% of all Ethereum coins in circulation to that point), making it the biggest crowdfund ever.

"The DAO" was meant to be an operating venture capital fund focusing on crypto investments. The actual breakthrough of "The DAO" was its organizational structure more than the fact that it tried to invest in crypto venture capital early on. The project was characterized by a lack of centralized authority to provide a lean and efficient organizational structure that gives control to investors rather than keeping it internal. Back when "The DAO" was still operating, any community member could pitch a project to receive funding from "The DAO". Token holders, in return, could vote and receive rewards for projects that became profitable.

While "The DAO" was initially doing well, it only took two months for the project to turn dark. On June 17, 2016, barely two months after the project was born, a hacker used a loophole in the code to drain the existing funds of the decentralized autonomous organization. 3.6 million Ether were stolen in the attack (worth more than 17 billion at Ethereum's all-time high of 4,891 USD and equivalent to around 70 million USD at the time of the attack). The hacker chose not to return the funds.

The intention of this book is not to get into the details of the attack. Still, for the purpose of curiosity and education, it is worth mentioning how the hacker managed to take advantage of the smart contract. In essence, he "asked" the underlying smart contract of the DAO to give back Ether multiple times before its balance was able to update. The code did not consider the possibility that a recursive call could happen. Equally severely, the smart contract first sent Ether funds and only then updated the internal token balance. The underlying issues were within the smart contract of "The DAO" and were not related to the code of the Ethereum blockchain as it only functioned as a foundational layer.

What followed the attack is history, leading to probably the most famous Ethereum fork yet. With the community acting fast, the hacked funds could be placed into a 28-day holding period. Intense community discussion led to the hard fork of Ethereum and Ethereum Classic. The new Ethereum fork returned the lost funds by sending new Ethereum tokens to those affected by the attack. The token owners were given an exchange rate of 1 Ether to 100 DAO tokens - the same rate as the initial offering.

Following the attack, there was a lot of backlash from the community and anger about how the newly forked Ethereum "violated" the idea of autonomy, but also fear how the attack would impact a move from Ethereum's Proof-of-Work (PoW) to Proof-of-Stake (PoS).

Not only that, but also the US Security Exchange Commission (SEC) showed interest in the project. According to the SEC, "Tokens offered and sold by a 'virtual' organization known as 'The DAO' were securities and therefore subject to the federal securities laws. The Report confirms that issuers of the distributed ledger or blockchain technology-based securities must register offers and sales of such securities unless a valid exemption applies. Those participating in unregistered offerings also may be liable for violations of the securities laws."

While the story of "The DAO" is not too glorious, it represents a crucially important building block for future development within the space. Due to the SEC ruling, crypto start-ups started using the SAFT method (Having a legitimate utilitarian value on a blockchain platform is violating a component of the Howey case[2], which means it cannot be applied. This is stopping them from being listed as securities). Additionally, Ethereum's hard-fork created the Ethereum that we know today (*more or less*) and Ethereum Classic. Most importantly, though, the concept of a decentralized autonomous organization stayed and lived on.

While we have spent some time learning about the history of DAOs until here, we have yet to better understand what DAOs actually are and the different types of DAOs that exist.

Within the crypto space, most people will have heard the word "DAO" at one point or another. "DAO" are communities with a common cause and an often-shared crypto wallet. While this might sound romantic, DAOs have exploded in size over the last few years and play a key role within crypto. Some of the most significant projects are run as decentralized autonomous organizations, managing tens of billions of US dollars.

Considering their importance as a foundational layer within the crypto space, we should dive deeper into what DAOs are, how they work, their strengths and weaknesses, and reflect on recent developments.

---

[2] The Howey four-prong test to be used in determining whether an "investment contract" exists is: (1) an investment of money, (2) in a common enterprise, (3) with the expectation of profit and (4) to be derived from the efforts of others

DAOs are at the core of the web 3.0 ecosystem. The goal is to create a decentralized, trustless governance structure that can operate without the need for a centralized decision-maker.

We can define them DAOs as follows:

"Decentralized Autonomous Organizations are blockchain-based structures that enable the coordination of people and resources through a formalized, transparent, and binding set of rules deployed on a public blockchain in a decentralized way"

Key characteristics of DAOs

- *In their purest form, they operate "autonomously" and are thus self-governed, meaning they are, amongst others, free from the oversight of any judiciary or law enforcement.*

- *They are decentralized and built as smart contracts on a blockchain.*

- *They are borderless due to their decentralization, with a flatter hierarchy and an often-formalized governance that is enforced on the blockchain.*

- *They own a treasury of (crypto) funds, allowing them to vote for transactions on-chain, reward contributing members, and invest in the development of the DAO, among others.*

There are different types of DAOs for different purposes. There are those that focus on building projects, those that focus on investments, those that aim to collect NFTs, those that provide services, and many more.

Protocol DAOs

The first category of DAO we should touch on is the so-called protocol DAOs. In essence, they are designed to govern a decentralized protocol (such as decentralized exchanges and DeFi applications, amongst others). Uniswap, a famous example of a protocol DAO, uses its governance token UNI to give community members voting rights. As such, the fact that Uniswap is structured as a DAO allows community members to decide on key changes in parameters, tokenomics, the treasury, and many more. However, voting power is not based on wallets but the weight of governance token ownership. This means that someone owning 20% of the governance token will be able to contribute 20% of each vote. At first glance, this might already seem problematic, and we will explore later on why that might be the case.

Grant DAOs

Grants DAOs fulfill the function of facilitating non-profit work within the crypto space. Their design allows non-profit organizations to deploy capital - supervised by the smart contract and managed by the members of the DAO. AAVE, the DeFi protocol, runs a community-led Grants DAO to fund ambitious developers and their ideas, helping them develop projects that can help grow the AAVE protocol.

Philanthropy DAOs

Similar to Grants DAOs, a philanthropy DAO focuses on charitable work. However, this work does not have to be linked to a specific protocol but can contribute to any philanthropic course, such as contributing to the UN Sustainable Development Goals. For example, Big Green DAO, the first philanthropy DAO, focuses on sustainable food, nutritional security, and climate impact.

Social DAOs

Social DAOs, don't focus on social causes but on the community aspect of DAOs. They aim to bring together like-minded people. Social DAOs can be behind NFT projects, or creative projects, thus having a small but meaningful barrier to entry. Friends with benefits, a social DAO that aims to "build a community and foster creativity," has a barrier to entry of 75 FWB tokens. However, members can attend exclusive events and connect with like-minded people once admitted. As such, Social DAOs derive much of their value from exclusivity and collaboration.

Collector DAOs

As the name suggests, the aim of collector DAOs is to collect. Community members participate in collector DAOs such as FlamingoDAO to collectively invest the treasury of the DAO in art collectibles, rare wine, blue-chip NFTs, the United States Constitution (ConstitutionDAO was remarkably close to doing so), and other so-called "collectibles" that can be found at auction houses. As such, collector DAOs are a way to invest in expensive projects without risking large amounts of personal capital.

Investment DAOs

Investment DAOs aim to invest in the DAO treasury. "The DAO" was the first example of this, and learning from their mistakes, new DAOs grew over the year with the same mission. The goal is to pool capital into a DAO treasury and invest in blockchain-focused venture capital on- and off-chain. The objective is to give retail investors access to investments usually unavailable in traditional financial markets.

Media DAOs

Media DAOs focus on creating content driven by the community. This is in contrast to how many news media are run today, as they usually have a top-down approach with senior management (or even politicians) deciding the content of the news medium. One such DAO is BanklessDAO, which is a community-driven DAO that focuses on driving the adoption of a "bankless money system." Decrypt is another example of a Media DAO, which allows community members to vote on the content rather than dictate it.

Service DAOs

Service DAOs can be best described as talent allocators. With the help of on-chain credentials, service DAOs allocate resources from one DAO to another. Service DAOs can cover a wide range of areas, be it marketing, treasury management, or something completely different.

Sub DAOs

Sub DAOs don't appear in the graph above; there is a reason for that. While they are separately presented for the purpose of this book, they represent subsets of the DAOs mentioned above. These subsets are · organized to manage specific functions such as operations, partnerships, marketing, treasury, and grants - they do not represent a separate kind of

DAO. Sub DAOs allow for more efficient organization of decentralized autonomous organizations.

Figure 15: DAO Landscape - A wide variety of DAOs exist with blurry lines between them

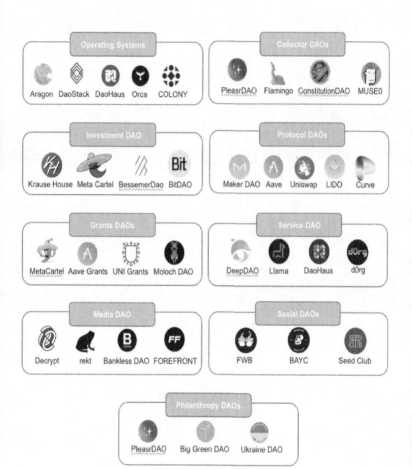

Compared to more traditional LLC structures, it is easier for a DAO to take on responsibility and create innovation - at least in theory. In reality, DAOs - at least for the time being - have to find a balance between decentralization and efficiency. A consequence of this was the creation of SubDAOs, pods, guilds, and so-called functional committees that aim to bring a more classical organizational structure into a DAO.

We can see that traditional organizations have a hierarchic structure that is generally closed and static. Transparency is close to none, and decision-making happens behind closed doors. Even a slight improvement here can go a long way.

The improvement we've seen with early DAOs is a shift toward a more open and transparent structure. DAOs have evolved from a monolithic to a modular structure, allowing for more specialization and scalability through delegation from a ParentDAO to smaller, more specialized SubDAOs. The delegation, in general, plays a critical role as it helps to overcome low participation rates. As such, despite the overlap between DAOs and traditional organizational structures in many aspects, key differences come into play when looking at the design aspects of DAOs.

DAOs often also lack formal managers, and membership can be anything but long-lasting. Members might join for a limited period and exit a DAO as fast and as easily as they joined. Looking closer at the management of DAOs, we can observe that an increasing number of DAOs are managed by what you could call a "distributed consensus" - essentially smart contracts that aggregate votes for decision-making.

DAO membership can be achieved in multiple ways. A more "traditional" approach would be a share-based approach. The share-based system allows the share-owner to participate in the DAO and vote on issues. As of late, a more common approach to membership is token membership. Token membership - while still envovles some hurdles - is more openly accessible. Through governance tokens, holders can vote based on their relative ownership and participate in a DAO.

Since it is hard to "control" who contributes to a DAO, specific tools can be used to quality-control and quantify different types of contributions. For example, there can be DAO-specific metrics or bounties that can be used to achieve targets. They help to define a shared understanding of priorities and motivation.

A vital element of a DAO is its treasury, which helps to keep the organization alive. The treasury can have many uses, reaching from fundraising, rewarding contributions, to grants and investments. A very common way to design a DAO treasury is as a multi-signature wallet tied to a treasury committee, which can authorize transactions

While other areas within the crypto space gained a lot more attention and traction in the last few years, DAOs are of crucial importance to developing the space further, fostering progressive decentralization and efficient organizational design.

Figure 16: DAO Organizational Structure

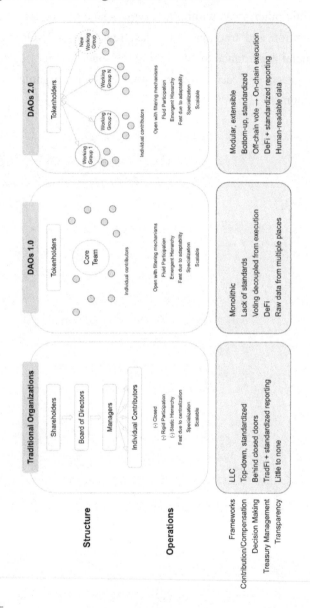

There are examples of two-token models where the governance of a project is separated from other aspects through the usage of two different tokens. Thus while one token allows us to govern a project, another token could be used for purchases or other noteworthy aspects.

Transparent and healthy governance can offer a lot of utility, drive the demand for a project, and lead to sustainable growth. Thinking about governance is also important, given the wish for decentralization and the aim of high participation rates of most protocols.

Considering the aspects of decentralization, it is vital to understand how much voting power is held by the team (and key investors) versus how much is held by the broader market. Projects that concentrate too much power in the hands of a team create an unfavorable environment despite adopting a DAO model.

However, we often see a gradual approach to decentralization with governance power being distributed out as community rewards are distributed over time. This allows projects to stay focused on implementing key changes in the early stages (when these changes are most crucial) and decentralize over time.

Having a closer look, we can observe that most projects operate in a similar way. As of now, most crypto projects choose to be organized in the form of a simple DAO structure, which comes with its own benefits and risks. The majority of these projects choose not only a DAO structure but also a "one coin, one vote" system, which can, in extreme cases, lead to plutocracy and low participation rates. To understand this better let us have a look at the basic DAO design.

Figure 17: Simplified DAO Design

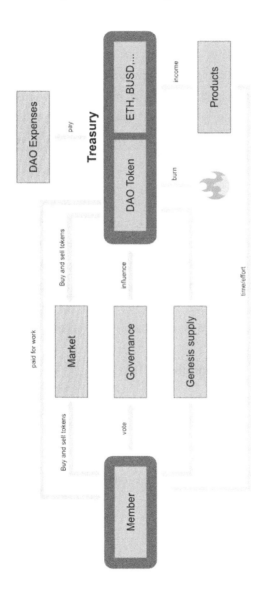

Over the course of the years, we have seen a second model gain in popularity. This model - the so-called vote escrow (ve) model - allows for higher voting power for locked tokens, helping to overcome one of the key downsides of DAOs - short-term governance participation. The aim of ve-models is to empower long-term holders by rewarding them for loyalty. The benefits here are obvious, as this model allows for more sustainable growth and could lead to less pump-and-dump of tokens.

Both these approaches (one coin, one vote, and vote escrow), generally speaking, help to coordinate communities, allowing for flexible and adaptive behavior compared to traditional organizational structures. As such, with a rise in the popularity of crypto and an increased number of projects building in the space, we could observe an increase in the total number of DAOs over the last few years.

Figure 18: Total number of DAOs

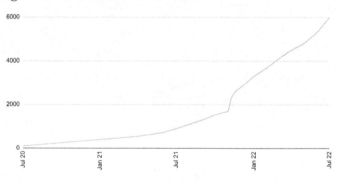

Source: Snapshot, Electric Capital

However, most governance models (so far) could improve when it comes to giving back value to token holders. For example, considering participation in a project, you are not rewarded more for a good decision compared to a bad one.

"Skin in the game", a concept first introduced by Vitalik Buterin, aims to connect the long-term success of a project to the votes that lead to it, thus aiming to overcome the problem mentioned above. The concept, first established in 2020, introduced a mechanism that holds each contributor in a decision individually accountable for their contributions. In essence, those who contribute to a good decision should get rewarded, while those who contribute to a bad idea should experience a more significant negative impact than those that did not contribute to the decision. While this is an exciting concept, we have not seen massive adoption as of now, though it should be something on top of the minds of projects building the future of crypto.

Nowadays, DAOs represent the backbone of the crypto industry as many - if not most - crypto companies are organized as decentralized autonomous organizations. There are a lot of exciting use cases for DAOs that go beyond the "*classic*" organizational structure.

Futarchy, a concept in which elected officials define measures of "national" well-being, and prediction markets are used to determine which policies will have the most positive effect, could be an interesting concept for the future. A meta-governance DAO that participates in multiple protocols could be another.

DAOs today are trying to solve some tough problems and reinvent the way we used to build and structure organizations since the start of the industrial revolution. As of now, DAOs are still in their infancy and have found a way to balance speed, efficiency, transparency, and decentralization.

Before concluding, it is important to remember that further development must occur for a healthy future for DAOs. Direct democracy is still at the center of DAOs and is slowing down the decision-making process when fast action and execution are most important. Furthermore, this form of democracy leads to low participation and concerns about weak oversight and centralized decision-making of a selected few. Overly concentrated voting in DAOs contradicts the goals of decentralization. As such, I welcome the development of subDAOs, working groups, and delegation as described above. As of now, it is still hard to find the right approach to what kind of decisions are suitable for DAO voting - clearly, not all might be.

Token Economy

W e have learned about Token Suppy and Demand as well as important governance aspects of tokens so far. Digging a bit deeper we should also pay close attention to Token Policy. Before doing this, I should first introduce the concept of a token economy. Understanding this concept well will not only allow builders to create sustainable projects and token economies, but also help to develop a framework for assessing the intrinsic value of existing projects.

Let's look at a common practice of a blockchain economy - producing and selling block space. In this scenario, the token policy is designed in a way that incentivizes validators to join the network to increase the overall security of the network. This, in return, allows people to feel more comfortable transacting within the ecosystem instead of using competing protocols.

Looking closer at the concept of token economy, we can observe that the productivity and reliability of an economy are key determining factors for how valuable that economy's currency is compared to others.

However, it is not easy for an economy's supply and demand to reach an equilibrium that enables efficient increase in the economy's size. According to modern monetary theory, this is where governments and central banks intervene and leverage monetary policy to optimize the balance of supply and demand.

Considering the growing popularity of Proof of Stake protocols such as Ethereum, hundreds of different projects in the market have tried to adopt a staking mechanism to encourage long-term token holding. Some of these projects created unsustainable staking yields, fueled by large emission rates to attract token stakers. These yields target one, and only one, objective: incentivize people to refrain from selling their tokens, though they often offer little other utility.

Additionally, for Layer 1 projects (and some Layer 2) to be usable and stable, their token economies must also fund "security expenses" by giving validation rewards. Two common sources include:

1. Transaction Fees from the network's users

2. Block Rewards or Staking Rewards (excluding transaction fees), which are freshly minted or released from the staking pool as incentives.

A complex set of objectives, including security level requirements, should be considered by any blockchain community deciding on its token policy. As such, the following framework provides a useful map of decision points in terms of subsidy rate and inflation.

Figure 19: Token Inflation Framework

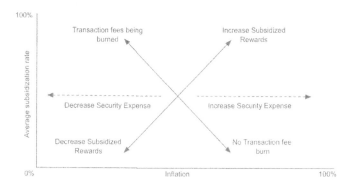

Consider this: if you have a token and want to reduce inflation or turn itself into a deflationary asset, burning all transaction fees will only help a little since block rewards most likely fund 98% of the security cost.

Therefore, the community can consider reducing or dropping the block reward to reduce the inflation rate, which is already baked into the token policy. In the future, when the block rewards are significantly smaller than now, the decision to start burning transaction fees would significantly reduce inflation, helping your project's token become a deflationary asset.

On the other hand, if the mining cost increases and profitability decreases, a drop in the number of miners might threaten the network's security. In this situation, the community can use the above framework to decide whether to increase block rewards or stop burning gas fees to keep the network up and running safely.

Two-Token Model

T o facilitate token economics, a two- and three-token model can be used to separate the functionality of tokens. Simply put, a two-token model provides two different tokens simultaneously, each with its own functionality and utility. This helps to specialize the use cases for each of the two tokens by separating an "*ecosystem*" from a "*purpose-solving*" token.

In most cases of two-token models, we have a utility token and a governance token. The utility token offers utility across most of the network to perform a specified task (e.g., to allow for in-game transactions). The other, helps to decide on the directionality of a project.

Governance Token

Governance tokens help to manage a protocol with the aim of not impacting the price of the utility token. This becomes important when considering use cases of a two-token model within games (amongst others) where the game design could be negatively impacted if a single-token model is used. If you want to make an in-game transaction (e.g. buy a collection item) but only have one token that is also used for governance, the game design might be negatively impacted due to speculation and price fluctuations. In extreme cases, this could lead to some gamers being excluded. As such, a governance token's main "task" is to help separate the management of a decentralized project from the remaining aspects that should be considered.

That being said, having a single token model is sufficient for a game that is truly focused on fun and entertainment. This minimizes confusion and dilution of in-game utilities and helps to concentrate market demand and market-making resources on one token.

Utility Token

This token is used only within the platform, network, or game. With this token, investors cannot raise funds as it serves specific purposes based on the platform's architecture. Utility tokens could enable specific actions or provide specific rights within a platform or GameFi project. The best way to think about utility tokens is to imagine them as in-game currency, where you wouldn't want to see large price fluctuations to exclude a huge majority of gamers and have an infinite supply to be able to scale the game without negative impacts from scarcity.

Figure 20: Pros and cons of a two-token model

Pros	Cons
Separation of use-cases	Token utility less concentrated
Unlimited supply of utility token	Unintentional correlation
No dilution to the governance token	Complexity

Evaluating the pros and cons, less dilution of the governance token is a key advantage. Conceptually, when a reward is given in a second token, we won't have a diluting effect on the first token. Furthermore, a separated utility token can allow for unlimited emissions, which is a key aspect to consider, especially for games. As such, a second token and a separation between governance and utility tokens can help control the utility token's inflation. This, in return, is important since you want to maintain a growing economy without leading to high barriers to entry due to high token prices. In addition, restrictions to having a fixed supply can be favored by investors since they are considering the price performance of a token. As such, separating use cases might help tailor a token to the right audience.

Despite the benefits a two-token model can bring, we must also note some negatives. Use cases of a token are separated - which can lead to unnecessary complexity. Furthermore, this complexity can lead to wrong expectations. So far, some investors expect tokens to be somewhat correlated where it shouldn't be the case, which can be seen when looking at the price movements of projects with two-token models such as Axie Infinity.

To overcome this, there could be an exploration of how a utility token should look like. Using stablecoins instead of a project-owned utility token might help to separate the price expectations of tokens. However, considering the stablecoin mechanism, risk and liquidity are important considerations to make.

Figure 21: Correlation matrix between SLP and AXS

	AXS	SLP
AXS	-	0.47
SLP	0.47	-

Source: cryptowat.ch
*Correlation: Positively correlated variables tend to move together
**Measured with first-differencing

As of now, we are still in the exploration phase, with different approaches to one-, two-, and three-token models. Depending on the use cases, each model offers some advantages and disadvantages. For gaming projects, the advantages outweigh the disadvantages regarding a two-token model.

The separation between governance and utility tokens comes with clear benefits that are important for games - such as inflation control and incentive through fixed supply for investors. However, we often observe net inflation of the secondary token, which could trigger a downward spiral. If the budget for initial rewards is fixed and subsequent rewards are funded by revenue in a controlled and calculated way, then inflation could be controlled. That being said, some areas should be explored further, such as the design of a governance and utility token in isolation from the other.

Vote Escrow

V ote escrow (also referred to as "ve") incentivizes liquidity providers to become long-term stakeholders. This is accomplished by granting increased rewards and governance powers to those who lock the underlying token.

Before the rise of veTokens, we lived in a world where many protocols rewarded all token holders equally, independent of the value they add to the project and their long-term commitment. As such, the vote escrow model rewards additive and long-term-oriented participants. To understand Vote escrow better, let us look at Curve, an early adopter of this model.

Curve is a decentralized exchange (DEX) for stablecoins, whose unique feature is its low slippage. CRV is the native token of the project, gaining utility by allowing it to participate in the protocol's governance. In order to participate in the governance of the protocol, users lock their CRV token to receive veCRV. Part of this governance participation is deciding how rewards should be allocated. A key demand driver for CRV is the number of people who want to participate in governance.

There are a few aspects that make Curve unique:

1. The longer you lock, the more vote-escrowed CRV (veCRV) you get

2. Locking is irreversible, and tokens are not transferrable

3. CRV lockers earn part of the protocol revenue

One utility aspect that the vote-escrow model brings to Curve tokens is to increase TVL without overinflating the circulating CRV supply. This effectively helps to buy time to grow the protocol, adoption, and revenue.

The ve-escrow model for CRV holders lets stakeholders lock up their tokens for up to 4 years. The longer users lock up their tokens, the more veCRV they receive. In addition to that, more veCRV will also give you more influence over emissions. veCRV holders receive a prorated share of fees generated by Curve.

Due to the long vesting period, instead of farming and dumping tokens, veTokenomics offered a new way to have skin in the game.

While the focus on long-term holding has been something many protocols tried to achieve and copy, there have been many variations of the original veTokenomics model - this can vary from early unlocks with a penalty to different approaches to vote gauge mechanisms.

Figure 22: Curve Model

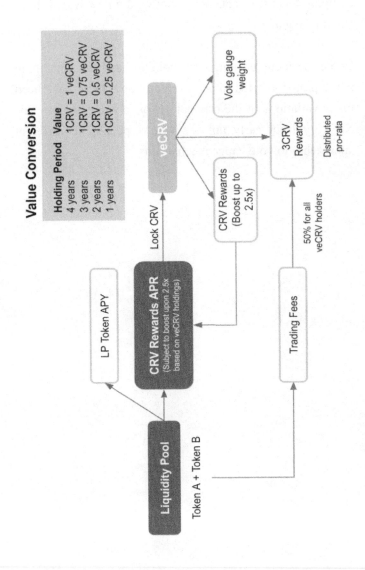

VeTokens help to incentivize long-term holdings. However, there are also some drawdowns to this model that we should be aware of. Long-term lockups make it harder for institutions and investors to participate, effectively reducing the governance base for the protocol.

While those that remain will likely be long-term oriented, the overall decrease in participation is still a drawdown. It is crucial to keep in mind that veTokenomics are not the perfect solution for every project.

Many projects suffered from high inflationary pressure and as a result underperformed compared to ETH and CRV. Since people realized that a one-size-fits-all approach does not work all the time, we have seen development in the space that we expect to continue. For example, Ribbon Finance allows early unlocking of veRBN with a penalty.

Non-fungible Tokens

There are many types of different tokens. One we should look at closer, considering its unique characteristics in a non-fungible token (NFT). Yes, you heard that right, a NFT is a token, too. The "*token*" part of an NFT means that like other "*digital assets*" such as bitcoin, Ethereum (other ERC-20 tokens), etc., an NFT is essentially digital code that contains certain information and that is created, stored, and transferred on a blockchain network. NFTs that exist on the Ethereum Network, for example, are traditionally ERC-721 tokens. Like all other cryptographic assets, the "*token*" part of an NFT cannot simply be copied or counterfeited. Furthermore, the creation and transfer of ownership of an NFT is recorded on the blockchain to which it belongs. If I buy an NFT from you on a given date, and that NFT was created on and exists on the Ethereum blockchain, a record of the transfer of that ERC-721 token will also exist indelibly on the Ethereum blockchain.

This means that at any given time, the owner of an NFT can point to the relevant blockchain and prove that they are the only owner of that NFT.

Every NFT differs from other NFTs, hence the "non-fungible" part of the name. To understand the non-fungibility of NFTs better, let us look at the characteristics of fungible tokens. Looking at Bitcoin, we can see the fungibility element in that every one bitcoin is functionally the same as another bitcoin. The Bitcoin you own is exactly the same that other people own. NFTs, however, are non-fungible in that two NFTs of the same collection are not the same and differ in their unique characteristics. In essence, Each NFT is distinct from every other NFT by virtue of a unique identification code and associated metadata embedded into the NFT when the NFT is created on its underlying blockchain.

Figure 23: Token Classifications

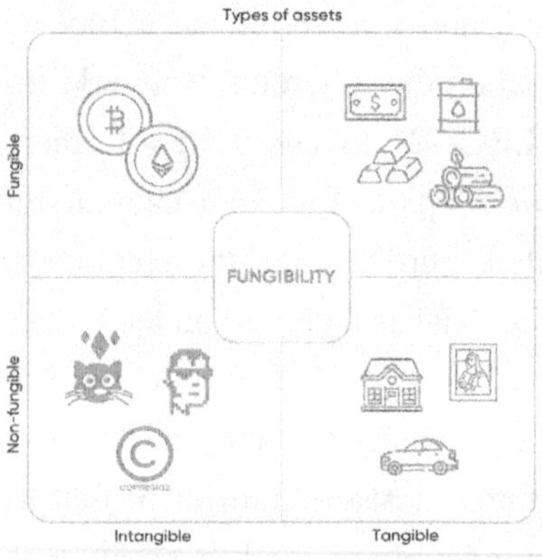

One important characteristic is that the unique identification code and associated metadata embedded into an NFT at creation are immutable and verifiable in the same way that the transactional history and record of ownership of blockchain "tokens" are immutable and publicly available for anyone to view and verify.

Another technical feature of NFTs is that NFTs are, by operation of their technical code, non-divisible. In contrast to cryptocurrencies, which can be subdivided into decimal fractions, NFTs exist on the underlying blockchain only as whole numbers.

Royalties

Another feature of NFTs that has been discussed extensively over the last year is that of "*royalties*". NFT royalties give artists a percentage of the sale price each time their artwork is resold. No matter how many secondary sales occur, the royalties will always be paid back to the original creator, and the best part is that the whole process is automated.

This is very different from the current way royalties work. Imagine you're a book author, and your books are being sold on the secondary market. Enforcing a form or royalty payment in perpetuity is almost impossible, leaving the author with no other choice but to accept the fact that he will not receive royalties from his copyright (yes, the struggle is real). In Web2, enforcement is even more difficult, as digital media is readily available and openly copied and transferred freely over the internet.

The amount of royalties each artist receives depends on the terms stipulated in the smart contract when the NFT was minted. Since the public ledger protects the integrity and authenticity of the artwork, the automated protocols will ensure that anytime the requirements specified in the smart contract are met, the relevant action is taken, which in this case is the payment of royalties.

That being said, some platforms have recently moved to 0% royalties, and time will tell if they will find adoption or not. These 0% royalties will ultimately lower the cost to "flip" an NFT and incentivize trading. However, with this, the project party has no source of funds for reinvestment. This might ultimately be bad for the sustainable development of the project party.

To counter this movement, token rewards-driven marketplaces such as LooksRare will no longer enforce royalties and instead pay creators a share of protocol fees. LooksRare charges a 2% total fee on the sale price, which means that 0.5% of the sale price will now be directed to creators in place of their respective royalty rates.

As such, the growth of zero-royalty marketplaces has eroded the general willingness to pay royalties throughout the NFT space. While this is good news for traders, the move away from royalties has removed an important source of passive income for most creators.

While NFTs began emerging as an asset around 2014, it wasn't until 2021 that their popularity soared. Chainalysis, a blockchain data analytics firm, released its 2021 NFT Market Report and reported that, in 2021, around 40 billion worth of cryptocurrency was sent to Ethereum smart contracts associated with NFT marketplaces and collections.

While NFTs are an extremely important building block for the whole crypto ecosystem and a key development, this book is not meant to dive deeply into the NFT space. As such, we will keep this chapter short concluding with discussing NFT use cases within games.

NFT Gaming

NFT games are different from the virtual collectibles that can be held in our wallets. They involve NFTs in the rules, mechanisms, and player interactions in the game. For instance, within an NFT game, a unique character, avatar, or virtual items like the weapons used in the game could be

NFTs. In contrast to the game owning the items, the player would be the rightful owner of a rare sword, bow, or armor. Players can then swap or trade these NFTs with other players to earn profits or obtain other rare items. The NFT game is created by implementing rules and conditions in a smart contract.

The collectible items have different values based on their cosmetics, rarity, or utility within the game. One example of in-game NFTs is CryptoKitties. They rely completely on the collectability of in-game NFTs. The latest NFT games offer both play-to-earn models and in-game NFTs.

Soulbound Tokens

After Vitalik Buterin, one of the co-founders of Ethereum, revealed that he too was a World of Warcraft fan, there has been an increasing discussion about so-called "Soulbound Tokens" (SBTs) within the crypto space.

SBTs build upon the concept of NFTs by removing the transferability element that characterizes today's ERC-721 smart contracts. The idea stems from the video game World of Warcraft, where some items can be "Soulbound" - e.g., players cannot sell or trade the items. Vitalik Buterin, Glen Weyl, and Puja Ohlhaver picked up that idea and brought it to the NFT space. Since their paper was first published in May 2022, we saw how the concept has slowly gained attention and adoption. However, as of now, the space remains in its infancy.

The problem we're trying to solve with SBTs is a dependency on Web2 infrastructure by introducing a native Web3 identity.

SBTs offer an (initially) publicly visible, non-transferable (but possibly revocable-by-the-issuer) token that can help to foster a decentralized society by creating an "immutable" record. This includes (but is not limited to) employment, work experience, and academic credentials and is thus offers a way to create a reputation on Web3. That's not to say that non-fungible tokens (NFTs) have not already offered a significant improvement in the way we exercise ownership over digital assets. It's more that their use cases are limited in aspects and don't help to overcome the dependency on Web2 per se.

Let's consider this:

- DAOs still depend on Web2 applications like Discord and Twitter to negate the possibility of a Sybil attack

- NFT collectors still depend on centralized platforms such as OpenSea to show the provenance of their collections

- DeFi platforms are limiting their offerings due to a missing trust element

SBTs could unlock benefits that can transform how we currently view social identities in real life, but also how crypto will evolve going forward. A user's identity should be portable across platforms, which helps to comprehensively build up their reputation in Web3. In addition to that, Soulbound Tokens can help to overcome the missing trust element and foster adoption, create clarity and promote transparency.

Design

SBTs are designed to be permanent, non-transferable tokens that allow individuals to verify their personal credentials (such as education, work history, and certifications) on-chain. Users can port their SBTs across various dApps to exhibit their verified traits. As of now, both ERC-20 and ERC-721 are transferable. SBTs, in contrast, are static and cannot be moved. This allows for a wide range of new use cases because it adds a new layer of functionality.

Figure 24: Differentiation between SBTs and NFTs

SBTs	NFTs
Non-transferable	Can be traded and transferred
Purpose of proof	Providing ownership
May allow for community recovery model	Almost impossible to recover
Can show provenance of an NFT, DeFi, etc.	Cannot show provenance themselves

While non-transferability is the primary differentiating factor between SBTs and NFTs, it is not the only one. SBTs and NFTs offer different use cases. While NFTs provide proof of ownership, SBTs offer proof of credentials.

Guardians

We all know the risks of losing access to our wallets. While losing access makes NFTs almost impossible to recover, there can be design aspects of SBTs that could allow for a recovery model. For example, a social recovery method that takes advantage of so-called guardians (this could be individuals, wallets, or institutions) could help to reset a private key. As of now, there are certain operational risks to overcome first, though. Social recovery wallets - while in theory a great way to secure a wallet long-term - force you to maintain a close relationship with your group of guardians.

As such, Vitalik's current view is that this system is best implemented not by curating guardians but by determining a "*maximally broad set of real-time relationships*", such as participation in protocol governance, a DAO, or memberships to communities.

Figure 25: A Community Recovery Model

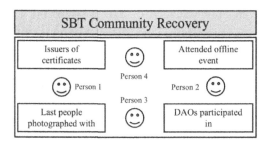

NFTs, while being on the blockchain, don't show provenance per se. This, however, is different for SBTs, which can show provenance.

As previously demonstrated, the design of an SBT should satisfy specific product requirements and the type of credential that the token encompasses. When building an SBT, there are multiple aspects to consider.

1. **Issuance** – SBTs should be easy to setup and provide high performance and scalability.

2. **Acceptance** –Since SBTs are public, users should have the ability to accept any SBT issued proactively. This prevents problems where an issuer could spam the user with an SBT they don't want, or a bad actor could issue the user an SBT that could harm someone's reputation.

3. **Control** – There can be special use cases for non-rejectable issuance of SBTs where the issuer has more control over the particular SBT-based reputation system. In those cases, users cannot easily wipe out an undesirable record to forge their reputation. Furthermore, since SBTs are often attestations from the issuer about the user, an issuer needs the ability to remove their attestation at a later time if it's no longer valid or true.

4. **Expiration** – It's quite common for assertions to have an expiration date that needs to be supported and should be considered in the design of an SBT.

5. **Discoverability** –It should be possible for third parties to discover which accounts have particular SBTs.

6. **Queryability** –It should be possible for third parties to easily query a given address to determine which Soulbound tokens are attached to that address.

7. **Trust** –Anyone viewing a user's SBTs should have trust about who issued the token, that it was issued to the user, and that it is still valid.

Use Cases

Outside of the BAB Tokens KYC, we have other use cases of SBTs that we should discuss in more detail. Although it seems that the current use cases are quite limited, let us have a look at the potential that SBTs could offer. The use cases for SBTs are wide-ranging and complementing the current NFT landscape. To understand the benefits of SBTs. Let us explore this in more detail.

Figure 26: SBTs Use Cases

While Soulbound tokens hold appeal for their ease of quickly conveying facets of a person's identity, the concept of on-chain tokens representing personal identifiable information (PII) raised some early concerns due to the immutable public nature of distributed ledgers. However, many of these early concerns were considered, and with users being able to remove SBTs from their profile, they're given a chance to decide which credentials they want to show.

NFT Ownership

One advantage of SBTs that facilitates the current NFT landscape is their ability to show provenance of NFTs. Currently, the Web3 space still relies on centralized businesses such as OpenSea, which introduces several risks. Furthermore, benefits introduced also include designing the prerequisites for minting in a way that only wallets with a specific SBT can mint an NFT collection. We could also think of a "lifelong" DAO or Community membership, where membership is granted through holding an SBT, proving specific qualifications or actions performed on-chain.

DeFi Lending

Benefits on the Decentralized Finance (DeFi) side are far-ranging. Currently, the majority of DeFi lending platforms, such as AAVE Protocol, do not always offer new services due to the hostility of highly private decentralized environments. This is where SBTs come in. By leveraging a user's interactions with different communities, DeFi protocols could move closer to offering new financial products to retail users. SBTs already allow proving interaction with a project, enabling "user sophistication". Together with the proof of KYC credentials, a lot of new avenues open up for DeFi protocols and the interaction between CeFi and DeFi.

Sybil Resistance Attacks

Sybil Attacks are a key concern for DAOs, limiting their growth and adoption. As such, Sybil attacks are the most notable system risks in coin voting within a DAO. To understand Sybil attacks consider the following scenario: If an individual accesses more than 51% of DAO tokens, the individual could gain control over the protocol. SBTs could help in solving the challenge through a representation of voting rights in DAOs. The non-transferable nature of SBT ensures that no particular individual can buy the tokens required for a Sybil attack. In addition, SBT can also ensure the transfer of voting rights to only those members that have an SBT credential proving some skill, academic credentials, and endorsement from other members.

Souldrops

It is one of the common practices for crypto projects to launch airdrops alongside general token sales. However, the process is generally associated with Sybil attacks, with whales consuming most of the drops. SBTs can potentially solve the problem by facilitating airdrops based on designed prerequisites and prior analysis of SBTs.

Academic Credentials

Universities, colleges, and schools can use SBT as digital proof of attendance or academic credentials for students. As an important set of non-transferable NFTs, they can help in verifying the credentials and proof of attendance of candidates.

GameFi Credentials

SBTs can help automate onboarding and expertise checks in GameFi apps by creating and recording a history of on-chain work and experience. From a game design perspective, you could limit access to specific levels and items to only those that have been airdropped an SBT proving the completion of a quest or similar.

Digital CV

Furthermore, SBTs can also offer the opportunity to create a unique digital CV. SBTs can act as verifiable endorsements to help prove that an individual has the necessary skills for the job. The non-transferable NFTs would ensure that professionals in different fields would have a publicly verifiable digital CV. As a result, it would be easier for employers to make hiring decisions based on the SBT a candidate has from their previous employers or academic institutions.

DAO Governance

One promising use case for SBTs is DAO governance. For example, Soulbound tokens can be used to implement one-person, one-vote rules or to enforce on-chain voting requirements for specific proposals. Furthermore, they can help DAOs, and other token-gated communities track applicants' experiences, skills, achievements, loot, and earnings across the whole metaverse.

SBTs are still in their early stages of adoption but show a lot of promise already. Not only do SBTs enable the creation of better trust relationships in decentralized environments, but they also offer significant improvements to protocols. These improvements are far-reaching, from improving the voting mechanisms within DAOs to offering improvements to the DeFi and NFT space. I forecast two major developments for Soulbound tokens.

1. Increased Adoption

While SBTs have played a minor role as of now, we expect this to change. Initiatives like the BAB Soulbound token introduces new ways for DAOs to fight Sybil attacks and for projects to Airdrop. As such, we expect adoption to be driven from a protocol level rather than a user level. Once enough projects have started using SBTs, we will likely see a shift towards retail users driving growth to qualify for airdrops, NFT minting, and other incentives. Originating from World of Warcraft, we see SBTs also returning to Games, with GameFi platforms so far not fully utilizing the potential of SBTs. Further growth of the Metaverse and GameFi space could drive fully crypto-native games that utilize SBTs to a greater extent. Within both these segments, the growth of SBTs will likely follow the overall growth of the space.

2. Regulatory clarity

Regulatory certainty is a great way to drive further adoption, and we believe that it will become important for regulators to address privacy concerns once the space gains enough substance. We believe that General Data Protection Regulation will be at the forefront of the debate but are confident that already existing design aspects help to ensure that SBTs exist within this regulation.

CBDCs

Central bank digital currencies (CBDCs) are the digital form of a government-issued currency that is not pegged to a physical commodity. They are issued by central banks, whose role is to support financial services for a nation's government and its commercial-banking system, set monetary policy, and issue currency. Around 90 countries, representing more than 90 percent of global GDP, are exploring CBDCs.

CBDCs are in many ways similar to stablecoins. However, while stablecoins are a specific type of private, stabilized cryptocurrency (frequently) pegged to another currency, commodity, or financial instrument with the goal of maintaining a relatively stable value over time, CBDCs are state-issued and operated and often not pegged to a physical commodity.

With CBDCs still in its early days, various approaches are being piloted. One type of CBDC is an account-based model, with consumers holding deposit accounts directly with the central bank. At the opposite end of the spectrum is China's e-CNY, a CBDC pilot that relies on private-sector banks to distribute and maintain digital-currency accounts for their customers.

The European Central Bank exploring a model in which licensed financial institutions each can operate a permissioned node of the blockchain network as a conduit for the distribution of a digital euro.

Token-based CBDCs

Token-based CBDCs use a digital token, and access and claims require users to have knowledge of the token. This approach typically offers a high degree of anonymity; however, central banks can choose to implement identity requirements to use the network. Token transfers rely on the sender's ability to verify the validity of the payment object and therefore require a form of distributed ledger technology for verifying the chain of ownership in each token and validating payment transactions. This also means higher end-user risk of losing a key or token held in a noncustodial wallet. In a token-based approach, commercial banks would need to be the first line of defense for compliance with know your customer (KYC) and anti-money laundering/combating the financing of terrorism (AML/CFT) regulations. This method can provide universal access to CBDCs but also makes law enforcement more challenging compared with other designs.

Account-based CBDC

Account-based CBDC access and claims are linked to a bank account tied to the identity of the account holder. This method is challenging for universal access because it still requires a banking relationship. To transfer funds, banks would process each payment by debiting the sender's CBDC account and crediting the beneficiary's CBDC account. Transactions need to be verified using user identities, and therefore, robust identity management systems are required to maintain a unique identifier per individual across payment systems. In an account-based approach, compliance with KYC and AML/CFT regulation is the responsibility of the central bank. Verification of transfers in an account-based system depends on establishing appropriate safeguards against identity theft, fraud, and unauthorized transfers from valid accounts.

Benefits and Risks

Before exploring the risks of CBDCs, we should first touch on some benefits. One of the greatest benefits is that CBDCs (similar to other cryptocurrencies) can improve access to finance for those without bank accounts. According to the latest data from the World Bank, as of 2021, there are an estimated 1.7 billion adults worldwide who do not have access to a bank account or any other type of formal financial institution. This represents about 22% of the world's adult population. The majority of the unbanked population lives in developing countries, particularly in Sub-Saharan Africa and South Asia, where access to financial services is limited due to factors such as a lack of infrastructure, high transaction costs, and low levels of financial literacy. The lack of access to formal financial services can have significant economic and social consequences, including limited access to credit, lower levels of entrepreneurship, and difficulties in saving and planning for the future.

CBDCs accessible through mobile devices could potentially increase financial inclusion. And for providers of digital financial services, mobile money presents a gateway into untouched markets. However, adoption isn't a guarantee; many underbanked people may favor total anonymity afforded by cash or other cryptocurrencies such as Bitcoin.

In addition, CBDCs could potentially enhance payment security by ensuring that a transaction is finalized and unalterable (even without a formal bank account), reducing the chances of fraud. Furthermore, regulated use of private-key cryptography could enable users to "sign" transactions digitally, reducing the wait time for a transaction to be irreversibly final and giving the parties greater peace of mind.

Central banks in some developed countries, such as Canada and Singapore, have concluded that there isn't currently a strong case for digital currency. I would even go one step further and argue that there are more reasons speaking against the use of CBDCs than for it.

In many ways, CBDCs are the government's attempt to protect its privileged position and exert more control over people's money. The real danger in CBDCs is that there is no limit to the level of control that the government can exert over people if money is purely electronic and provided directly by the government. A CBDC would give federal officials full control over the money going into–and coming out of–every person's account. This level of government control is not compatible with economic or political freedom.

Instead of focusing on building CBDCs, governments should foster more access to financial markets and ensure more innovation in financial services by supporting more private innovation and competition. They should reduce government monopoly and regulation and forgo issuing retail CBDCs.

While it's still too early to predict what the future holds for CBDCs, we should be careful about the amount of control it gives to central banks and the benefit of (potential) financial inclusion should be weighed against the risks that CBDCs bring. In many ways, CBDCs are often dismissed as a solution in search of a problem.

Wide adoption of CBDCs will create a dramatic change in how much data is generated by everyday transactions. If the wrong technology is chosen, we could end up with a state - even a democratic one - that knows your identity, your income and your transactions, holding even more power over your life. As such it is important to review and publicly discuss which features of the CBDC would promote financial inclusion best, how the CBDC can ensure a reasonable level of account and transaction anonymity, and how generated data will be processed, stored, and eventually destroyed.

Token vs. Shares

Key takeaways from this section…

- *Tokens capture the economic output of a given project, whereas the value of equity captures free cash flows*

- *Inflationary supply does not need to be bad if the business grows with it.*

- *Evaluating crypto businesses like stocks is not enough - and can be often misleading.*

- *If the business is good, governance tokens can be a proxy.*

W E can view tokens as a key way for users to participate in a project. This is slightly different for Venture Capital (VC) firms as they often have to decide between equity or token ownership in a crypto-native company. The same holds for projects looking to raise capital, with a key question on their mind being whether to raise funds in the form of a token or through equity ownership, whilst allowing investors to have a share in the company behind the token.

As a retail investor or fund participating in tokens on the secondary market, you will often look at the key mechanisms of token supply and demand as outlined in the previous sections and try to understand the overall token utility.

When thinking about tokenomics from a VC perspective, however, other elements should be considered.

Both, tokens and equity can be great ways to raise capital. They both help to attract and retain talent, represent ownership and allowing us to measure the value of the underlying project or business. Furthermore, both can be managed in ways to increase or reduce supply and tokens.

However, there are key differences, and **the equity value is not equal to the value of tokens**. As such, classic valuation methods such as using a traditional discounted cash flow (DCF) method, often don't work well when considering tokens. The reason for this is manifold. One key element, though, is that tokens capture a given project's economic output, whereas the equity value captures free cash flows.

As a VC investor who believes that blockchain is the technology of the future and is likely to power much of the Web3 world, most of the value created will reside in tokens. This, in return, allows investors to capture value creation directly. Furthermore, it will enable them to generate yields on their ownership and play a significant role in Network governance and decision-making. That being said, there will be many blockchain companies where a token may not offer any utility and the value created does not reside in tokens. For most of these projects, an equity investment makes more sense from an investor's viewpoint.

Governance

Let us look at a few elements to better understand the difference between equity and tokens. One is that of governance. Publicly listed companies are governed by a board of directors. This board decides on key decisions within the company, such as electing the CEO, the remuneration, the issuance of new shares, or the buyback of outstanding shares.

Within the crypto space, this looks different and as mentioned in previous chapters, DAOs often play a key role in the governance of crypto projects. Looking at the most common "one token, one vote" model, token holders fulfill the function of a board of directors, having the power to vote on issues related to the project, such as electing a CEO, as well as the issuance of more or less tokens (that is, if the project is using a DAO structure and is not centralized).

Often the issuance of new tokens is programmed into the smart contracts of a protocol or encoded within its mechanisms. A famous example here is Ethereum's EIP-1559. Fundamentally, EIP-1559 removes the first-price auction as the main gas fee calculation.

In first-price auctions, people bid a set amount of money to pay for their transaction to be processed, and the highest bidder wins. With EIP-1559, a discrete "base fee" for transactions will be included in the next block. Users who want to prioritize their transaction can add a "tip," which is called "*priority fee*", to pay a miner for faster inclusion. In theory, the more transactions that occur, the more deflationary pressure the burning of the base fee will have on the overall Ethereum supply - but more about it later.

Comparing governance between crypto and traditional businesses, we should also mention regulatory concerns. Within classic cooperations, shareholders have certain rights that they can execute. This includes a claim to a corporation's assets in case of liquidation (with ordinary shares being served last). Looking within the crypto space, this often isn't the case. While there is more flexibility for token holders, protection is often neglected (at least for now).

As a token holder, you generally have some form of decision power over a treasury that receives protocol revenues. However, if not written in code, you don't have a direct claim on that revenue, and it might stay within the treasury without being distributed to token holders.

Token ownership

Next, let us look at token ownership in isolation before diving into equity ownership.

If you're a young project aiming to sell tokens to investors, you must first decide what you seek to tokenize. This can include multiple things. For example, you might want to tokenize present (or future) utility, a governance right, or the right to receive a share of future profitability. In the next step, you will need to lay out your tokenomics and value proposition and decide on the supply and "price" of your tokens when giving them to venture capital firms.

In the next step, selecting an appropriate blockchain platform for the project to be deployed on is crucial. It is important to ensure that appropriate security protocols are in place, that a token wallet is established, and that smart contracts are defined to govern token sales and receipt of payment.

In terms of the actual token sale, there is typically a pre-sale promotional campaign to stimulate as much interest in the token as possible. The sale window can last weeks – but is usually completed within hours – and investors are ordinarily required to pay for tokens in either fiat or cryptocurrency.

Issuing tokens can offer many benefits. Tokens can offer a lot of flexibility in terms of design and programming mechanisms, making them a very flexible tool. They can further help to incentivize certain outcomes better than classical equity can by allowing for time-based vesting mechanisms and innovations in terms of voting rights.

Tokens are often more predictable, considering that the logic and mechanisms can't be easily changed. While this removes a lot of arbitrary human action, it also has its downsides. Having a programmed mechanism that burns tokens or controls the vesting period can often lead to not-so-great timing issues. Having a vesting period or buyback that happens in periods of high volatility and/or in a bear market can add another layer of pressure on the token that the project might fear. The same can happen when a project is clearly overvalued, but the pre-determined mechanism doesn't allow for flexibility in terms of buying at a later price when the price might be lower. Having a clear understanding of how these mechanisms work and impact the token flow is important when evaluating tokenomics.

Considering the multiple layers, evaluating a token is a lot more complex than assessing a business. In equity research, it is only a secondary consideration to evaluate the shares (and share structure) as a majority of work goes towards assessing the company. When entering the space of cryptocurrencies, it is not only necessary to evaluate the business itself, but also the tokens as well as the supply and demand characteristics of it.

A common ratio that people look at is the price-to-sales ratio. However, considering that tokens function quite differently to shares, we should look at this ratio in more detail to illustrate some key differences.

Price-to-sales ratio - *The price-to-sales ratio compares the fully diluted market capitalization with the annualized total revenue of a project.*

Because crypto projects often use tokens as an incentive mechanism, they risk running into sustainability issues. As such, while the price-to-sales ratio might look good, token emission needs to be considered to create a more consistent image.

Equity ownership

As mentioned earlier, a key element of what makes stocks valuable is the underlying business and, less so, the shares' design. As a shareholder you "own" part of the business, which in itself represents some form of value. Many companies pay dividends to shareholders to create additional motivation for holding the stocks, as they distribute parts of the revenues.

If the underlying company doesn't pay a dividend, the main value of the stock comes from ownership of the underlying business. If you believe that the company is set up for growth and will be worth more in the future the value of your underlying stock will increase if the market agrees with you. Profits are thus not paid out but reinvested into the company. In this case, ownership means owning assets, intellectual property, and earning power.

Simply put, the performance of your equity ownership is strongly dependent on the performance of the underlying business. In a worst-case scenario, many traditional businesses also hold tangible assets that can be liquidated (though traditionally, shareholders are paid last). When evaluating a "traditional" business, analysts often look at past earnings, costs, and investments made to determine the future earnings power of a company.

Key Metrics in accessing traditional companies:

Price-to-earnings (P/E) ratio

The price-to-earnings ratio is quite possibly the most heavily used stock ratio. This ratio tells you how much investors are willing to pay for a stock relative to its per-share earnings.

Computing the P/E is simple: Divide the stock's share price by its earnings per share (EPS). For example, if a stock has a P/E ratio of 20, investors are willing to pay up to 20 times its EPS to own it. But is that too much or too little? Expensive or cheap? Ultimately, it can depend on what a company can accomplish in terms of future earnings[3].

---

[3] You can compare a stock's P/E to that of the S&P 500 historical average return, which was almost 12% over the last 10 years (assuming dividends are reinvested). During the bull market that began in March 2009, the index's P/E ranged from 13.5 to nearly 124, ending at about 23 in March 2020. The limit to the P/E ratio's effectiveness is that it can't really tell you much beyond what investors are willing to pay for the stock now.

Price/earnings-to-growth (PEG) ratio

The price/earnings-to-growth (PEG) ratio can provide a more comprehensive and clearer picture of a stock's future growth prospects. With the PEG ratio, you're comparing the P/E to the analyst consensus estimate of projected earnings.

The PEG is derived by dividing the P/E ratio by projected EPS growth. For example, a stock with a P/E of 18 and a percentage growth rate of 15% would carry a PEG of 1.2.[4] When buying shares with a low PEG ratio, investors tend to look for a history of growth in combination with projected growth, which can help validate an undervalued PEG ratio.

Price-to-sales (P/S) ratio

The price-to-sales (P/S) ratio shows how much investors are willing to pay above a company's gross revenue, whereas investors focused on earnings are looking at revenue minus liabilities. Revenue may not be considered as "solid" a figure as earnings for a valuation, but sales are generally subject to less manipulation by management than earnings numbers.

---

[4] Typically, stocks with a PEG ratio of less than 1 are considered undervalued.

Although earnings can be affected by various expenses, what a company makes in sales is quite straightforward.

The P/S ratio is calculated by dividing the stock price by sales per share. For example, a firm with $500 million in sales with 100 million shares outstanding would post sales per share of $5. If the stock price is $10 per share, the P/S ratio is 2.

Price-to-book (P/B) ratio

The price-to-book (P/B) ratio indicates how much a company's stock is worth relative to its net asset value (also known as book value). On the surface, it's an effective metric that can compare a stock's market capitalization to what it owns versus what it owes. But it's not always that simple. Figuring what a company's assets are worth can be a big sticking point. To find a company's real book value—which also is called "shareholders' equity"—you might have to dig a lot deeper, beyond the books. The P/B ratio is best suited to large, capital-intensive companies, such as automakers, rather than companies with intangible assets, such as software firms where much of the value is based on patents or other intellectual property that's not carried on the books as an asset.

Debt-to-equity (D/E) ratio

The D/E ratio is seeking to find out what a company owes relative to what it owns. The calculation is simple, and the figures for a firm's total debt and shareholders' equity can be found on the consolidated balance sheet.

A high D/E ratio indicates a company has borrowed heavily. Generally, investors prefer the debt-to-equity (D/E) ratio to be less than 1. A ratio of 2 or higher might be interpreted as carrying more risk. But it also depends on the industry. Big industrial energy and mining companies, for example, tend to carry more debt than businesses in other industries. That's why investors typically compare a stock's D/E ratio to the D/E of other companies in the same industry.

As many crypto companies are very early stage and growth-focused, it is hard to assess them based on profits, and public information is often hard to find.

Profit participation right

With profit participation rights, there is any freedom of design as to what the investor receives:

1. A *defined share* of the company's profit

2. A share in the profit of a *defined part* of the company

3. A share in a *differentiated defined* cash flow

Individualized co-determination rights and combinations with rights of use and other incentives can often be agreed upon. Within the equity space, which had a long time to develop and mature, different and flexible structures such as profit participation right investment can be found. This allows equity investors to participate in the profit participation rights. Profit participation agreements may outline each party's interest percentages, accounting obligations, and dispute resolution procedures.

Security Token Offering

Security Token Offerings (also known as STOs) bring together the world of equity and cryptocurrencies. A Security Token Offering is the initial sale of tokens to raise funds for the project's activities (most often related to cryptocurrencies). However, instead of offering utility tokens, investors get the deed of ownership of a given property in exchange for an investment (As such, their token ownership represents a security token rather than a utility token). The fact that STOs are similar to securities puts additional regulatory oversight on them. STOs effectively combine blockchain technology with regulated securities markets' requirements to support the liquidity of assets and the wider availability of finance.

STOs bring together the benefits of blockchain for financing in a regulated environment, with the possibility of exchange-based and asset-backed structures increasing potential appeal. To be sold as a security to investors, the requirements under applicable securities laws such as the Securities and Futures Ordinance (Cap. 571) (SFO) in Hong Kong or the Securities Act of 1933 in the United States must be met. Besides securities laws, issues such as transferability, electronic transactions obligations, custody regulation, insurance, and stamp duty can also arise.

> **Key Elements of STOs**
>
> - *Security tokens are similar to analog securities. By tokenizing illiquid assets such as private company shares, real estate, or intellectual property rights, the original owner of the illiquid assets can monetize such assets in whole or in part through an STO with much lower transaction costs.*
>
> - *The STOs are subject to existing securities regulations in many jurisdictions, including the US and UK. However, it is still not common for major securities exchanges to launch an STO.*

There are three types of STOs that we should be aware of. These include

1. Asset-backed Tokens

Asset-backed tokens represent ownership of assets, such as real estate, art, carbon credits, or commodities. Being secure, immutable, and transparent, blockchain enables a trusted record of transactions and reduces fraud while improving settlement time. This makes blockchain technology a natural fit for commodity trades. Asset-backed tokens are digital assets with characteristics like any commodity, such as gold, silver, and oil, which, in turn, bring value to these traded tokens.

Developers building resource-based investment tokens most often use Ethereum blockchains.

2. Equity Tokens

Equity tokens are similar to traditional stock, except for how ownership is recorded and transferred. Equity tokens are secured by shares or the company's capital. An equity token is recorded on an immutable ledger and offers benefits regarding a company's decision-making, financial outlook, and regulatory frameworks. For example, equity token holders are entitled to a portion of the firm's profit and have a right to vote. In addition, startups have access to new and, potentially, more democratized fundraising models. Equity tokens are secured by either

3. Debt Tokens

Debt tokens represent a short-term loan on an interest rate, in the amount investors give as a loan to a firm. They thus represent financial debt instruments such as corporate bonds, loans, or real estate mortgages. A debt token's price is dictated by "*risk*" and "*dividend*". The reason for this is that a medium risk of default can't be priced the same for a real estate mortgage and a bond for a pre-IPO organization.

In terms of blockchain, a smart contract lives on the network, representing debt security. Repayment terms are included in that contract, dictating the underlying debt's dividend model and risk factors.

The growth and future development of STOs comes in the form of their role to foster permanence, security, and transparency. When thinking about securities, each element is imperative to confidence, trust, safety, market efficiency, and soundness. The emergence of security tokens does not stop with only liquidity and revenue distribution frameworks. Instead, security tokens open a lot of new possibilities for investments. Small investors of specific security tokens could sell off either the dividend portion of full equity or a small part of their interest in a secondary market. In addition to that, by combining the existing infrastructure with decentralized autonomous organizations, it becomes possible to code voting choices into their smart contracts.

As mentioned above STOs often fall under the definition of securities in most jurisdictions, and we should thus look at this element in more detail. While the definition varies from jurisdiction to jurisdiction, the well-known US Howey Test provides a foundation for general understanding. Building on a case in 1946 between the Securities and Exchange Commission (SEC) in the USA, and Howey, two Florida-based corporations, the Howey test is a functional test as to whether an investment is a security and thus subject to the U.S. securities laws. The four elements include:

1. It is an investment of money or other forms of assets
2. There is an expectation of profit from the investment
3. The investment of money is in a common enterprise, meaning that investors pool their assets together to invest in a project
4. The profit comes from the effort of a promoter or third party, which is entirely out of the investors' control

Security tokens are generally assumed to meet these since they represent a share of an issuer's profit or cash flow, or their assets are very likely to fall under the definition of securities.

Benefits and Drawdowns of STOs

Given the characteristic of security tokens, an infinite number of tokens can be issued, and large numbers of investors can own the assets. Furthermore, STOs offer an opportunity to make illiquid tangible and intangible assets tradable, thus increasing liquidity. STOs further allow the flexibility to fractionalize the illiquid asset into smaller tradable fractions in the form of tokens, similar to asset-backed securities.

Using smart contracts allows for storing key specifications, such as valuation reports or authentication proofs, and making them available to all investors. Since the information is stored via distributed ledger technology, fraud risks should be reduced through the central design features of permanence, transparency, and security. This also applies to real estate, where the owner might sell a portion of its rental income without going through a complex listing such as a Real Estate Investment Trust (REIT).

That being said, STOs are still relatively new, and adoption is still low due to exchanges fearing the scrutiny that comes with listing securities. Nonetheless, security tokens are here to stay, and more security tokens will undoubtedly launch soon. As blockchain technology attempts to revolutionize the financial space, the STO market is indeed one to watch in the coming years.

Looking at the benefits closer we can crystalize three main benefits.

1. **Saving time and money** – Compared to classical IPOs the time it takes to get started and run a successful STO is usually much shorter. Thanks to STO's, it is possible to raise money in a cheaper, and more effective way.

2. **Global reach and availability** - STO's huge advantage over traditional solutions is the use of technology that allows you to attract investors from every corner of the world. The benefit is that STO tokens tend to be more liquid than other types of assets.

3. **Ownership** - Tokens issued under STO most often represent shares in the project, and this allows voting rights and profits from the startup's revenues.

STOs, however, are not flawless. Like any method of fundraising for startups, STOs have several disadvantages.

1. **A higher entry threshold** - To become an investor through STO, you must meet the legal requirements related to identity verification and have no administrative contraindications to invest. This, of course, also raises higher legal costs.

2. **Presence on the crypto exchange** - To trade security tokens, owners must wait for them to be added to the cryptocurrency exchanges. In the case of smaller projects, this expectation can be quite long.

3. **Young market** - One of the most important factors distinguishing IPO from STO is the fact that the IPO has existed for centuries. In contrast, security tokens have only been issued for several years. This means that not all aspects of the new market have been fully tested yet, and therefore investing in this type of project may be burdened with a much greater risk.

There are numerous reasons why STOs are still at a relatively early stage of development. Although an increasing range of digital asset intermediaries, market infrastructure providers, issuers, and promoters are subject to regulation, certain activities related to the crypto business remain unregulated. (*for example, P2P exchange services and decentralized exchange services - that promote buying and selling of tokens - mining pools, and cloud mining services - which facilitate the mining of crypto-assets*).

Without generalized protocols or legislation, investors might experience loss or ambiguity when executing trades. Even though actual assets often back Security Tokens, the valuation for virtual assets remains difficult. With uncertain liquidity, accounting professionals have difficulty ascertaining the fair value of the Security Token. And due to the unique design and structure of each Security Token, it is difficult to find a referencing token for valuation.

Initial Coin Offerings

An initial coin offering (ICO) is the cryptocurrency industry's equivalent of an initial public offering (IPO). A company seeking to raise money to create a new coin, app, or service can launch an ICO as a way to raise funds. In contrast to STOs, ICOs are often not registered as securities, although some have subsequently been determined by the SEC as investment products.

When a cryptocurrency project wants to raise money through an ICO, the project organizers' first step is determining how they will structure the coin. ICOs can be structured in a few different ways, including:

1. **Static supply and static price** - Setting a specific funding goal or limit, which means that each token sold in the ICO has a preset price, with the total token supply being fixed.

2. **Static supply and dynamic price** – With a fixed supply of tokens and a dynamic funding goal, the amount of funds received in the ICO determines the overall price per token.

3. **Dynamic supply and static price** - A dynamic token supply and a static price lead to the amount of funding received determining the supply.

It is important to remember that in an ICO, a coin holder might not necessarily have a claim to any assets or cash flows of the company. Furthermore, the lack of regulation also means that someone might do whatever it takes to make you believe they have a legitimate ICO. As such, an ICO is one of the easiest ways to set up a scam and prior due diligence is important when investing in an ICO. Most ICOs go hand-in-hand with the publication of a whitepaper detailing the idea of the project.

Initial Exchange Offerings (IEOs) are ICOs that list directly on a virtual asset exchange. Crypto exchange trading platforms stepped in to fill the role of traditional securities distributors and play to conduct due diligence services on the crypto asset to ensure the credibility of the project. That said, the IEO still needs to address the fundamental concern of the stability and credibility of the coin itself, especially since the coin is not backed by underlying assets. Hence, the value is highly subject to speculation.

There are a few risks related to ICOs that I want you to be aware of. These include but are not limited to the following:

1. **Idiosyncratic risk -** Typically, ICO projects are at a very early stage of development, and their business models are experimental. Thus, the value of the investment is uncertain.

2. Liquidity risk - The possibility to trade or cash in the acquired token on a platform may be limited due to low liquidity.

3. Fraud risk - Some companies may potentially intentionally make use of collected funds or virtual currencies in different ways than promised

4. Inadequate documentation - ICOs often only offer a whitepaper. This whitepaper is not subject to any legal norms, and therefore may be incomplete or misleading.

5. Insufficient transparency - Investors do not obtain any impression about the company or the development of the project. It is often necessary to have a complex technical comprehension to be able to understand the features and risks of the ICO in its entirety.

6. No investor protection - There is no deposit guarantee scheme and no legal investor protection.

7. Lack of supervision - ICOs are not subject to any kind of regulation or supervision. Legal enforcement may be significantly hindered to the extent of being rendered impossible.

ICOs vs. STOs

ICOs and STOs are based on asset tokenization. In both cases, tokens represent the value that is emitted – though the similarities end here. Comparing ICOs and STOs, we see that the biggest difference is the legal requirements. Almost anyone can start an ICO, and you do not need to comply with dozens of regulatory provisions associated with traditional fundraising methods to complete this process.

On the other hand, STOs are strictly governed by the laws and regulations of the jurisdiction in which it is held. Moreover, an investor buying tokens actually becomes a shareholder of the startup. Hence, STO is often described as a compromise between an IPO and an ICO.

Figure 27: Comparison STO vs. ICO

	STO	**ICO**
Risk	Lower risk	Higher risk
Convenience	Not so convenient for token issuers. Investors need to pass regulatory checks.	Easy for both the token issuers and investors. Once the right platform is available, less effort is needed for the ICO sales.

	STO	**ICO**
Regulatory requirements	Higher levels of regulatory scrutiny	Uncertain
Growth potential	A lower investor base and backers can be limited based on the underlying regulations.	ICOs can be very successful as there are typically no boundaries to the investor base.
Limitations	Time required to complete regulatory checks.	Low level of limitations
Cost Factors	Relative	Relative
Challenges	Each firm has its unique challenges.	Project diversity would bring a different challenge.
Development platforms	Relative	Relative
Public Exchange Listing	STOs are listed on trading platforms under the regulatory oversight of the market regulator in the country.	There are dedicated cryptocurrency exchanges where the underlying assets from ICOs can be traded.

Considering the growth of STOs and the advancement in the space, the difference between tokens and equity becomes smaller and smaller. As such, evaluation as to whether or not a project is sustainable boils down to similar considerations. Is the founder's financial incentive aligned with the value creation or not? What is the competitive edge of the project and is it likely to generate cashflows and profits in the future?

It is important that investors and builders look at both the business and the mechanisms of the token. The token and its mechanisms make things a little more complex, which requires us to evaluate both. If we do, crypto projects might be run more like businesses, and we could see more sustainable tokenomics emerge.

Initial Dex Offerings

An initial DEX offering (IDO) is a fundraising approach that pools investment capital from retail investors. IDOs were originally created to compensate for the shortcomings of the "traditional" ICO crypto crowdfunding model. Because an IDO uses a decentralized exchange, as opposed to a centralized exchange, we can also think about DEXs as decentralized *liquidity* exchanges.

By using the decentralized exchange, projects can market their tokens to the public and allow investors to lock their funds in the smart contract before the projects launch their native tokens

While decentralized exchanges have been around since 2012, utilizing hashed time-locked contracts (HTLCs), it wasn't until the start and growth of Ethereum that we saw them take off. The introduction of Ethereum smart contracts fueled a new generation of exchanges and introduced prolific improvements over HTLC-based exchanges. In 2016 Vitalik Buterin proposed what would become the key foundation for today's decentralized exchanges (DEX). Uniswap, launched by Hayden Adams, was one of the first projects that implemented Vitalik's idea to employ an on-chain automated market maker (AMM) with certain unique characteristics. Today, DEXs have become a pivotal element in the crypto world and a key building block of DeFi applications by enabling trading with considerable improvements in crypto volume. While some DEXs were already up and running using classic order books, it really was the introduction of automated market makers that brought broad popularity to DEXs due to their simplicity and increased liquidity.

Today's decentralized exchange lets you transfer various digital assets on an open market with no middlemen. As such, they have almost all of the capabilities of a centralized exchange but stand out for their ease of exchanging the myriad of currencies that are accessible online.

There are two main types of DEX to be aware of: order-book-based, and automated market makers.

1. Order Book DEXs

An order book is generally made up of buy-and-sell limit orders from market participants. The market price for an asset is the lowest asking price (sell order) or the highest bidding price (buy order). Placing a market order means a trader would buy or sell at the market price instantly, taking away liquidity from the order book, hence they also often pay a taker fee. This order book matching mechanism essentially matches active buyers and sellers at a specified price, providing more control to traders.

Some popular order book DEXs include LoopRing and Gnosis Protocol, which both use an algorithm to find trades between individual users, and smart contracts record the exchanges on the blockchain to reflect the coins and tokens that are moving between buyers and sellers.

Order books can be on-chain or off-chain. On-chain order books have their order placement, matching, and settlement engine done on-chain, with transactions verified by validators. For on-chain order books, index prices are often determined by validators who would act as price oracles, submitting last traded prices from various exchanges to the chain.

Off-chain order books, on the other hand, use off-chain logic2 to handle trades, transactions, liquidations, index prices, and so on. Order books are most suitable for an exchange where the liquidity is high. That's because they help maintain low slippage irrespective of the trading volume. Conversely, in illiquid markets, traders must wait for long times, which results in more exposure to market volatility and large spreads.

2. Automated Market Maker DEXs

Decentralized exchanges such as Uniswap utilize what is known as an "automated market maker" model. The key reason for their existence is the poor performance of order books in illiquid markets.

The advantages of this model are straightforward. From an efficiency perspective, AMMs offer very low spreads, but at the same time, they only require a blockchain transaction for actual trades, not placing or canceling orders. Furthermore, this is an overall simple design in terms of implementation, which can lead to increased efficiency and transactions per second.

Automated market maker-based DEX replace the order book with a liquidity pool. This liquidity pool is basically pre-funded by the users who are known as liquidity providers (LPs). Thus, instead of matching buyers and sellers, the trades on AMM DEXs are carried out using liquidity pools managed by a smart contract. Liquidity is "sourced" from users who essentially give their tokens (in trading pairs). Every AMM-based DEX incentivizes the LPs in a different way. Off-chain logic handles trades, liquidations, transfers and deleverages, as well as updating the oracle prices. It stores the entire balance of all the users, and periodically submits proofs, attesting the validity of the balances change, given the user's transactions.

To get a better understanding of the AMM model, let us look at Uniswap in more detail. Long before Uniswap, EtherDelta was probably the most used decentralized exchange. This changed, however, in November 2018, when Uniswap v1 was launched on the Ethereum Mainnet. In Uniswap v1, trades were made against liquidity pools, and a mathematical formula determined the price of assets, with liquidity providers adding liquidity to the pools that help to make a market. Uniswap v1 actually only supported the swapping of ETH-ERC 20 pairs, making trading a bit more complicated than it is today. Uniswap v1 also facilitates the concept of LP tokens. The simple idea behind this is that LPs add liquidity to any pool, and they receive LP tokens representing the added liquidity.

Uniswap v2 launched in May 2020 and, you guessed it, got rid of the painful ETH bridging, that made v1 less user-friendly. With v2, we finally had ERC20-ERC20 pools that boosted a lot of growth in the DeFi space. Some other innovations that came with Uniswap v2 included the concept of flash swaps, which allows users to withdraw any amount of ERC20 tokens without having to pay upfront. Users could either pay for the tokens withdrawn or pay for a portion and return the rest or return all the withdrawn tokens. Another noteworthy innovation was that of protocol fees. A protocol fee of 0.05% of the total 0.3% trading fee was now reserved for the development of the Uniswap platform.

Uniswap v3, when compared to v1 and v2, provides better capital efficiency and accuracy. Instead of just picking an equal value of two tokens, you can now select your preferred fee tier in any liquidity pool. By default, Uniswap provides three fee tiers you can choose from. Uniswap v3 also introduced liquidity concentration, which means that you can set a certain price range where you provide liquidity. This is a way of decreasing your impermanent losses. To understand this better, let us look closely at how Uniswap v2 worked. Within the prior version of Uniswap, liquidity was distributed evenly along an x*y=k price curve, with assets reserved for all prices between 0 and infinity. This means that most of the liquidity is sitting unused instead of rewarding LPs for taking the risk of impermanent loss.

The idea that Uniswap v3 introduced is that a position only needs to maintain enough reserves to support trading within its range, and, therefore, can act like a constant product pool with larger reserves (virtual reserves) within that range. Liquidity providers can create as many positions as they see fit, each in its own price range. In this way, LPs can approximate any desired distribution of liquidity in the price space. Moreover, this serves as a mechanism to let the market decide where liquidity should be allocated. Rational LPs can reduce their capital costs by concentrating their liquidity in a narrow band around the current price, and adding or removing tokens as the price moves to keep their liquidity active.

Since LPs can provide liquidity in custom price ranges, their liquidity positions in Uniswap v3 aren't fungible anymore. Another key improvement that Uniswap introduces in v3 relates to Oracles. Uniswap v3 introduced significant improvements to the time-weighted average price (TWAP) oracles. It's storing an array of cumulative sums instead of just one like Uniswap v2 did, thus making it possible to calculate any recent TWAP within the past nine days in a single on-chain call. This improvement makes it easier to create more advanced oracles easier and cheaper. Uniswap claims this will reduce the gas costs for keeping oracles up to date by 50%.

There are many other benefits that v3 brought to Uniswap, but at this point, you might be better off reading the Uniswap v3 whitepaper directly.

Figure 28: Comparison AMMs and On-chain Order Books

Automated Market Makers (AMMs)	On-chain Order Books
Usually market orders only, but other order types are slowly getting popular	Many types of orders, such as limit, stop loss, trailing, buy-stop, etc.
Can have high slippage if liquidity is low	Can have high slippage if liquidity is low, but reduces the risk of slippage by setting limit orders.
More ideal for illiquid markets as liquidity is present at any price and trades will always be filled	More ideal for liquid markets and not for illiquid markets as a trader's limit order may not always be filled
Risk of front-running via MEV or sandwich attacks	Lower risk of front-running if measures are taken
Liquidity providers risk impermanent loss	Off-chain liquidity providers do not risk impermanent loss
Do not require oracles to determine price	Prices are usually determined by external market makers

For projects issuing their tokens on an AMM, we can see how can provide traders with the ability to directly exchange their assets from the liquidity pool. The prices are increased and decreased based on the assets in the liquidity pool. It is important to note that the pricing may vary simultaneously depending on the assets which are listed in the centralized exchange.

IDOs work because DEXs can provide immediate token liquidity. Therefore, DEXs tend to reward liquidity pool providers with handsome rewards. And as we have seen above, liquidity allows DEXs to operate without any unexpected hiccups for their users.

To assist with trading, most projects provide liquidity to the DEX by allocating a cut of the funds. This approach has become standard practice. Circumventing the rigorous approval process has granted many projects access to retail investors. The same can be said about avoiding the high cost of initial exchange offerings (IEOs). On the downside, IDOs also make it easier for many poor-quality projects to list. Such projects also include scams.

In addition to that, DEXs remain vulnerable to technical exploits. IDO often don't require a sign-up, and there is no KYC, or any other relevant policies are present. Anyone can participate, become a member, and own a part of the project without revealing their identity.

Does a company need a Token?

W hy does a company need a token? Well, the simple answer is, it doesn't. The more complex answer is that many benefits can come with tokens, but at the end of the day, a strong product is always more important than having a token - not all projects have a token, and not all need a token.

However, some projects have a good token design that is not working in reality. Let's uncover the dynamics between product, design, and token in more detail.

Product is key. Always. It is a plus if a project raises funds through an ICO or STO and offers an attractive token design. Good token design can incentivize growth and lead to interest alignment between the project, its investors, and users. Having a good token design but a bad product will, however, ultimately remove demand and lead to a downward spiral. In the long run, good projects with strong fundamentals will always win over those with bad fundamentals, and good token design cannot be seen as a long-term solution to keep a project alive.

OpenSea is an example of a crypto-native project with a good design, strong competitive advantage, and no token. As one of the first established NFT trading venues on Ethereum, OpenSea's competitive advantage has been its first-mover advantage and strong adoption, as well as its very intuitive UI/UX design. OpenSea supports over a dozen crypto wallets, with MetaMask and Coinbase Wallet being the most popular.

While decentralization is a central tenet of the crypto space, OpenSea can look a lot like a Web2 company operating in the Web3 space. Rather than distributing its fees back to users or giving users the option to vote on business decisions, as some marketplaces do, OpenSea operates like a typical Silicon Valley company.

One of the big "disadvantages" of OpenSea is its strong centralization which generally goes against what many are looking for within the crypto space. Thus, despite the strong competitive advantage of OpenSea, we have seen how more decentralized projects such as Blur and LooksRare have gained market share and traction.

The NFT exchange LooksRare started a vampire attack on OpenSea, showing us how projects can use token incentives to grab significant market share from a market leader in a short period of time. During the launch of LooksRare, 12% of the total token supply was airdropped to OpenSea traders, luring them to try LooksRare and move from OpenSea to their platform (in the early days, volume on LooksRare surpassed that of OpeanSea). LooksRare's airdrop is an example of a tokenomics design that focused on "stealing" market share from the leader in a short period of time. Despite early success, it remains to be seen how sustainable such an approach can be. Development in market share suggests that it might not be too sustainable, and the world of NFT marketplaces still needs to find its leader.

Blur airdropped its BLUR governance token to NFT traders who earned rewards through the marketplace, and also by trading elsewhere ahead of Blur's own launch last fall. Blur has incentivized traders to treat NFTs more like DeFi tokens, flipping frequently and attempting to maximize every potential benefit through liquidity mining.

OpenSea isn't the only project that operates a successful crypto business without a token. MetaMask and Arbitrum are just two other famous examples that don't have a token (yet).

In 2019 Ed Felten, the co-founder of Offchain Labs, famously said: "There isn't an Arbitrum token, and we don't expect to create one. Contracts on Arbitrum can use any Ethereum-based token they want. We decided that we didn't need to create yet another token." As such, answering the often-asked question of "Wen Token?" sometimes has to be answered with a simple. "When it makes sense".

One key reason for these projects to potentially create a token over time is to bring progressive decentralization to the project. It is important, though, to do it over time and in ways that are meaningful. We should create real decentralization where possible and empower people. In contrast, we should avoid creating tokens out of greed.

Combined with smart contracts, tokens allow for credible and meaningful representation of metered resources in digital form, including voting rights, licenses, land rights, securities, and physical assets. As public blockchains gain acceptance as legitimate global sources of truth, the costs of representing real-world ownership in digital form become smaller when built on this common infrastructure. This translates to lower transaction costs, which will in turn accelerate e-commerce.

Risks & Challenges

Key questions to keep in mind when reading this section…

- *Does this project need a token? (You can ask this from both a founder and investor perspective)*

- *What is the link between the protocol and the token? Is there a reason for the token to accrue value in relation to the protocol?*

- *Does the project have competitors? Do they have tokens? How are they performing and why?*

As we have learned, just because you can issue a token for your project does not mean that you should, or even that you need to. Issuing a token is a difficult and complicated endeavor and not one that should be taken lightly. As mentioned, a strong product is key and should definitely be the major selling point of a project before delving into the world of tokens and tokenomics.

Once a project feels ready to implement a token there are still a few risks and challenges that are important to be aware of. In order to simplify the task at hand, we can consider dividing our subject matter into the following categories: fundamental risks, operational risks and legal & regulatory risks.

Fundamental Risks

These are key issues for both founders and investors to look out for in order to better understand any given situation involving tokens. Firstly, holistically speaking, why does this product need a token? What problem does having a token solve / what additional benefit does it provide, if any? The utility should always be at the center of any token, and it should become okay to operate in the Web3 space without having a native project token. If a token has no practical use case, it may not have any intrinsic value, and investors may end up holding worthless assets. The absence of a clear use case for a token can lead to a lack of demand for it, resulting in low trading volumes and a lack of liquidity. This can make it difficult for investors to sell their holdings, leading to significant losses. Additionally, without a clear use case, the token may not have a sustainable business model, which can make it difficult for the project to attract ongoing investment and support. Therefore, it is critical for investors to carefully evaluate the utility and viability of any token they are considering investing in to ensure that it has a clear use case and a sustainable business model.

Secondly, issuing a token without having the final product in mind (and the roadmap toward it) can lead to long-term issues. Changing an existing tokenomics model is never easy and can have a negative impact on the business. As such, especially when creating a finite supply, you should have the finished product in mind. For investors, the future change to tokenomics and token use cases can represent a fundamental risk that is important to be aware of. It is important to have a clear rationale around the token issued and a clear utility assigned to it. Don't get me wrong, it is okay to be experimental. If you are at an early stage, you have enough room to pivot the product and token according to market needs – this could, of course, mean maintaining the ability to inflate your token (just like equity) to keep the operations going and raise money.

In the rush to launch a token sale and raise funds, issuers can sometimes lose sight of the underlying project. This can result in a lack of progress on the project and a failure to deliver on promises made to investors. Moreover, a lack of focus on the project can also result in a failure to build a community around the token. A strong community is essential for the success of a crypto project, as it can provide support, feedback, and evangelism for the project.

To mitigate this risk, issuers need to focus on the project itself and ensure that they are making progress on the development of the underlying technology. They also need to communicate effectively with their community and provide regular updates on the project's progress.

Companies must focus on creating a product that provides real value to their users before issuing a token.

Market Risk

One of the most significant risks associated with investing in crypto tokens is market volatility. Crypto markets are known for their extreme price movements, with prices rising and falling rapidly based on market sentiment and news events. This volatility can result in significant losses for investors, and it can be difficult to predict market movements.

For example, the volatility of Bitcoin, the largest and most well-known cryptocurrency, has historically been high. According to data from Coin Metrics, Bitcoin's 30-day volatility has ranged from 0.85% to 23.7% over the past five years, with an average of around 5%

Furthermore, crypto markets are also susceptible to market manipulation, as the lack of "*working*" regulation and transparency makes it easy for bad actors to influence prices. This type of manipulation can result in significant losses for investors and can damage the reputation of the entire crypto industry. The volatility of the cryptocurrency market can be attributed to a variety of factors, including market sentiment, regulatory changes, and technological developments. The lack of regulation and the relatively small size of the cryptocurrency market compared to more established asset classes also contribute to its volatility

Liquidity Risks

Finally, liquidity risks are another risk associated with tokens. Liquidity refers to the ease with which an asset can be bought or sold without affecting its price. In the case of crypto tokens, liquidity can be limited due to the lack of regulatory oversight and the limited number of exchanges where these tokens can be traded.

Furthermore, liquidity risks can also arise from the lack of demand for a particular token, which can result in significant price drops and difficulty in selling the token. This type of liquidity risk can be particularly challenging for smaller tokens that are not widely adopted

When comparing the liquidity of crypto tokens with traditional financial assets, there are several key differences. While the 24/7 trading and global nature of crypto markets can provide greater trading opportunities, misguided regulation and a limited number of exchanges can create liquidity challenges. Moreover, the extreme price volatility of crypto tokens can also impact their liquidity.

On the other hand, traditional financial assets can provide a higher level of liquidity. Traditional financial markets have a well-established trading infrastructure, including stock exchanges, brokers, and clearing houses, that help facilitate trading and ensure that trades are settled quickly and efficiently. Overall, the combination of well-defined rules and regulations, a larger number of participants, a wider variety of assets, and an established trading infrastructure all contribute to the greater liquidity of traditional financial markets compared to cryptocurrency markets (at least for now). Additionally, the ability to short-sell stocks and other traditional financial assets can provide additional liquidity and trading opportunities for investors.

Regulatory Risk

One of the most significant legal risks concerning crypto tokenomics is the lack of *clear* regulations. Governments around the world are struggling to define the boundaries of this new asset class, and this lack of clarity creates uncertainty for investors, issuers, and other stakeholders in the industry. This lack of clarity can lead to legal risks, including regulatory fines, lawsuits, and reputational damage.

Additionally, tax and accounting regulations are also a significant concern for crypto tokenomics. The tax treatment of cryptocurrencies varies from country to country, and the lack of clear guidance can make it challenging for individuals and businesses to comply with tax laws. As more businesses and individuals begin to use cryptocurrencies, regulators will need to provide clear guidance on how they should be taxed. Failure to comply with tax laws can lead to legal risks, including fines and penalties.

Another legal risk is the potential for intellectual property disputes. With so many new tokens being created, there is a risk of infringing on existing patents, trademarks, or copyrights. Issuers need to be aware of these risks and take steps to protect their intellectual property rights. Failure to do so can lead to legal risks, including lawsuits and reputational damage.

Finally, there is also the risk of regulatory action. Regulators may decide to impose new rules and regulations on the crypto industry, which could impact the value of cryptocurrencies and the viability of crypto businesses. Investors, issuers, and other stakeholders in the industry need to be aware of these risks and take steps to mitigate them.

Regulators also need to provide clear guidance and regulations to ensure that the industry can continue to grow in a safe and sustainable manner. Failure to do so can lead to legal risks, including fines, penalties, and reputational damage. As the industry continues to evolve, it is essential to remain vigilant and proactive in addressing legal risks concerning crypto tokenomics.

Classification Risks

Cryptocurrencies have been described as a new asset class that is neither a currency nor a security. However, as the crypto industry continues to grow and mature, regulators around the world are scrutinizing cryptocurrencies and the tokens issued on blockchain networks. This scrutiny has led to concerns that some crypto tokens could be treated as securities, which would subject them to stricter regulatory requirements and legal risks. We should thus also examine the risk of crypto tokens potentially being treated as securities, including the legal framework for determining whether a token is a security, the consequences of being classified as a security, and strategies for mitigating this risk.

The legal framework for determining whether a token is a security is based on the Howey Test, established by the US Supreme Court in 1946. The Howey Test defines a security as *an investment in a common enterprise with the expectation of profit solely from the efforts of others.* In other words, if investors are putting money into a project with the expectation of making a profit, and that profit is largely dependent on the efforts of others, then the investment may be considered a security.

The Howey Test has been applied to a range of investment vehicles, including stocks, bonds, and mutual funds. However, applying the Howey Test to crypto tokens can be challenging, as these tokens can have a range of utility functions beyond pure investment. It would be worth exploring migrating away from the Howey test long-term and finding a new evaluation framework that is more fitted for the drastic change and innovation that crypto tokens bring.

If a crypto token is classified as a security, it would be subject to regulatory requirements and legal risks. These requirements could include registering with the appropriate regulatory bodies, providing ongoing disclosures to investors, and complying with securities laws. Failure to comply with these requirements could result in regulatory fines, lawsuits, and reputational damage. Furthermore, being classified as a security could also limit the liquidity of the token, as it would only be tradable on regulated exchanges. This could make it more challenging for issuers to raise capital and for investors to exit their investments.

To mitigate the risk of crypto tokens being treated as securities, issuers can take several strategies, including:

1. **Utility Token Design** - Designing the token to have a primary utility function beyond pure investment can help establish that the token is not a security

2. **Clear Disclosure** - Providing clear disclosures to investors about the nature of the token and its intended use can help establish that the token is not a security

3. **Avoiding Expectations of Profit** - Avoiding marketing the token as an investment opportunity or making statements that could create the expectation of profit can help establish that the token is not a security

4. **Legal Opinion** - Seeking a legal opinion from a reputable law firm can help establish that the token

is not a security and provide a defense against potential regulatory actions.

The risk of crypto tokens being treated as securities is a significant concern for issuers, investors, and other stakeholders in the crypto industry. The legal framework for determining whether a token is a security can be challenging, and the consequences of being classified as a security can be severe. As the crypto industry continues to evolve, it is essential to remain vigilant and proactive in addressing this risk.

Operational risk

Issuing a crypto token involves significant operational risks that issuers need to be aware of. In addition to the technical challenges of developing a blockchain network and creating a token, issuers also need to manage treasury operations and focus on the project itself.

One of the most significant operational risks associated with issuing a crypto token is treasury management. Issuers need to be able to manage the funds raised through the token sale effectively. This involves managing cash flows, budgeting, and financial reporting.

Moreover, issuers also need to manage the cryptocurrency reserves that are used to back the token. This involves managing the storage and security of the reserves, as well as monitoring the value of the reserves to ensure that they are sufficient to back the token.

Failure to manage treasury operations effectively can result in significant financial losses, regulatory fines, and reputational damage. It is essential for issuers to have a clear plan for managing treasury operations and to work with experienced professionals to ensure that these operations are executed effectively.

Issuing a crypto token involves significant operational risks that issuers need to be aware of. Treasury management is a critical area that can impact the success of a token sale and the underlying project. Issuers need to manage treasury operations effectively and focus on the development of the project to mitigate these risks. By doing so, issuers can increase the likelihood of success and build a strong community around their token.

Token Velocity

A fter having looked at many crypto pitch decks it is fair to say that most if not all include one assumption: *If there is a fixed supply of tokens, the token price will increase in line with an increase in demand.*

However, reality is often more complex than theory and velocity is a key aspect we should consider when thinking about tokenomics. In some cases, a project's underlying token mechanics are not structured in a way that the price of the underlying token will materially appreciate with increasing demand.

Using the example of ticketing, we can make the reasonable assumption that a user would acquire project tokens as part of the ticket purchasing process. However, it is very unlikely that they are holding the tickets for the long-term as the utility aspect is low and incentive to help them and incur price risk even lower. Most certainly venues and organizers won't have a lot of incentive to hold the project token either, since they are having very similar incentives as retail users. Once a consumer converts a NFT or token for the concert ticket, the organizer will likely trade the underlying token for their preferred currency. As such, despite having utility in allowing for the purchase of the ticket and the transfer of ownership, the utility is not long-lasting since there is no long-term incentive to token holders.

> *The aspect of long-term incentive is crucial for projects and can come in many forms. This can reach from a discount for long-term vested holders for future purchases to revenue accrual from the ticket sales from the platform. The ultimate design is up to each project but important to be considered when designing tokenomics*

Taking our above-mentioned example one step further we can see how the introduction of a token can even add new and unnecessary complexity that worsen the overall user experience (UX).

A high trading volume for a well-established token can be misleading since it just indicates trading activity in a token and even with a ticketing-focused token that is market-leading the incentive for long-term holders remains low. Market makers, providing liquidity for those entering and exiting the market will likely have the time of their life, but they might be the only ones.

While token utility might be low, we should not neglect other benefits that blockchain technology can bring. Ticketing fraud can be reduced drastically bringing real value to consumers and organizers. Issuing tickets on blockchains can bring other benefits, including disallowing resale, profit sharing on resale back to the venue, capping resale amounts, etc. – the token's ability to capture of this utility is low.

Looking closer at the element of token velocity we can define velocity (broadly speaking) as the total transaction volume per average network value.

$$Velocity = \frac{Total\ Transaction\ Volume^*}{Average\ Network\ Value}$$

Total transaction volume includes not only volume that occurs on exchanges, but also over-the-counter trades and actual usage of the platform

Applying the outlined formula, velocity is 0 if nobody buys or sells the token making liquidity a key element to allow for fair pricing.

Don't get me wrong, assets need some velocity to achieve their full intrinsic value. The difference between fair pricing and full intrinsic value is known as the liquidity premium.

In the case of a proprietary payment token that nobody wants to hold, velocity will grow linearly with transaction volume.

In extreme scenarios, it could be theoretically possible for transaction volume to grow a million-fold, and network value could remain constant. Sadly, many tokens suffer from this problem.

Reducing velocity

So how to reduce velocity to a healthy level?

1. Introduce a profit-share (or buy-and-burn) mechanism

Examples of this include paying token holders for performing work for the network. Token holders on the flipside, need the token in order to qualify for the work. A profit-share mechanism reduces token velocity because as the market price of an asset decreases, its yield increases. If the yield becomes too high, market participants seeking yield will buy and hold the asset, increasing the price and reducing velocity[5].

---

[5] Also, a cash-flow stream makes a token easier to value using a traditional discounted cash-flow (DCF) model.

2. Build staking functions into the protocol that lock up the asset

This includes proof-of-stake mechanisms for achieving network-layer consensus.

3. Balanced burn-and-mint mechanics

While deflationary assets might bring some short-term price support there is a lot of reason to be skeptical of currencies that are explicitly deflationary to create upwards price pressure on the value of the token. In the long run, deflationary currencies will create weird incentives for holders, causing unnecessary volatility due to excessive speculation. The burn-and-mint mechanism addresses this problem (slightly).

In the long run, there should be a linear relationship between the usage of protocol and price.

ERC20 tokens do not have network validators who can be compensated via inflation. Burn-and-mint is possible for ERC20 tokens, albeit trickier. For one, there's not a generic set of network participants who should receive the tokens that are generated by inflation. In addition to that, inflation is tricky to implement because smart contracts cannot run as daemons that auto-inflate; they must be triggered.

4. Gamification

To encourage holding, gaming elements could be implemented, such as rewarding customers based on their token holding or on-chain activity.

One major reason for holding crypto assets is an expectation that they will increase in price. In theory, if this is the case, this should dampen velocity and drive up the price of the asset. Bitcoin is a great example of this since its value is a function of a speculative value game, not particularly from the intrinsic utility as a payment system.

In summary, token velocity plays a crucial role in understanding the behavior of participants in the cryptocurrency market. It is important for projects to have a good understanding of these elements. For so many things, here too having strong utility and use-cases is extremely helpful in order to improve token velocity.

Mechanism Design

One of the foundational results in mechanism design is the Revelation Principle. In essence, it states that any social choice function achievable through an arbitrary mechanism can also be achieved through a truthful, direct-revelation mechanism, resulting in the same equilibrium outcome. A direct-revelation mechanism refers to a system where individuals straightforwardly disclose their characteristics to the mechanism, which then determines a course of action and allocation of resources. A direct-revelation mechanism is considered truthful if it is dominant for individuals to faithfully report their preferences, although in some cases, this requirement may only hold in a Bayes-Nash equilibrium. Such mechanisms are often referred to as truthful, incentive compatible, or strategy-proof.

The revelation principle carries significant implications, granting tremendous power. In essence, if a proposition can be proven true within the scope of these mechanisms, it can be deemed true for all mechanisms. To understand why this holds, consider a hypothetical dishonest mechanism equipped with an interface layer. This layer interacts with the mechanism on your behalf, strategically manipulating your reported preferences to maximize your personal gain, similar to a fiduciary. Under these circumstances, it would be detrimental to misrepresent your true preferences to the interface, as it would lead to suboptimal rewards. Essentially, you need not lie, as the mechanism effectively lies on your behalf. The observation that there is no loss of generality by focusing solely on truthful, direct-revelation mechanisms is the pivotal result that enables the efficacy of mechanism design. Otherwise, one would need to prove theorems to be true for the vast array of indirect or dishonest mechanisms, rendering the subject practically futile.

Constrained Optimization

Now that we have established some fundamental concepts, let's explore the types of outcomes that can be enforced through mechanism design. What constitutes a "good" mechanism, and how can we ensure its selection? This can be approached as an optimization problem, where our aim is to maximize an objective function (such as revenue) while adhering to a set of constraints. Let's delve into some common constraints you are likely to encounter.

Incentive compatibility is a frequently encountered constraint. Alongside this, we have other commonly observed constraints, including individual rationality, which ensures that no participant incurs losses by engaging in the mechanism, and efficiency, which maximizes the overall sum of individual utilities (excluding monetary transfers). Budget balance imposes the requirement that the mechanism's transfers balance out to zero across individuals, while weak budget balance simply mandates that the mechanism does not pay out more than it receives. In the realm of mechanism design theory, a key challenge arises from the fact that constraints like budget balance, efficiency, and individual rationality are often impossible to simultaneously satisfy while ensuring incentive compatibility. As a result, several impossibility theorems have been established.

Generally, the characteristics of mechanisms can be evaluated ex-post (*irrespective of the agents' types*), ex-interim (*given any agent's type and the expectations regarding other agents' types*), or ex-ante (*expectations over both one's own and other agents' types*)[6].

---

[6] Drawing parallels to a poker game, we can think of the claims one can make before any cards are dealt (*ex-ante*), when aware of one's own hand (*ex-interim*), and when all hands are revealed (*ex-post*).

When we introduce constraints, mechanism design transforms into a constrained outcome optimization problem, often resulting in a range of potential mechanisms to consider. Let's take the example of an auction, where you seek an incentive-compatible and individually rational mechanism that maximizes revenue. Depending on your specific requirements, you may also need mechanisms that are computationally efficient or capable of achieving more intricate social objectives, such as equitable value distribution. These examples merely scratch the surface, as the possibilities are virtually endless. As we explore various examples, we'll observe that articulating the precise objective of a mechanism can itself pose a significant challenge within mechanism design.

Vickrey-Clarke-Groves Mechanisms

A frequently encountered and highly influential class of mechanisms is known as Vickrey-Clarke-Groves (VCG) mechanisms. To understand these mechanisms, let's consider an auction scenario where a single item is being sold. The straightforward approach might involve participants writing down the price they are willing to pay on a piece of paper. However, this design is not incentive-compatible since a player bidding their true value would end up with zero utility. A much better mechanism, ensuring incentive compatibility, is the Vickrey auction. In this setup, the item is allocated to the player with the highest bid, but they only pay the value of the second-highest bid. Each player has an incentive to bid their precise valuation for the item.

A generalized form of the Vickrey auction is the pivotal mechanism, also known as the Clarke mechanism or "the" VCG mechanism (although VCG can refer to a broader class of mechanisms). Here's how it works: For each individual, the mechanism is run without their participation, determining the outcome that maximizes the utility of all other players based on their reported types. Then, the individual is included, and the mechanism is run again, with the latter outcome being chosen. Each player pays or receives the difference between the sum of utilities for the other players in the two cases. This payment represents the individual's social cost or benefit. Since the individual cannot influence the sum of utilities that occurs without their presence, they effectively seek to maximize the sum of their own and everyone else's utility, which aligns with maximizing total social utility. By aligning incentives in this manner, the mechanism ensures not only incentive compatibility but also guarantees efficiency. It is relatively easy to find versions of this mechanism that are ex-post individually rational and weakly budget balanced, given some reasonable additional assumptions. Additional terms can be introduced to the payout that the individual cannot influence, such as providing a constant amount to each individual regardless of the outcome, without altering the underlying incentives. This more general class of mechanisms is referred to as Groves Schemes, which are always dominant strategy incentive-compatible. Notably, they are the only efficient mechanisms where truth-telling is a dominant strategy.

Applications

Now that we have assembled the basic ingredients from mechanism design, let's look at some potential applications to the cryptocurrency world.

1. Token Sales

Token sales represent one of the most evident and direct applications of mechanism design. Auction theory stands out as the most extensively explored domain for applying mechanism design principles. If you are considering a token sale, you can discover readily available solutions by delving into the realm of mechanism design. However, it is worth noting that as we progress, we will encounter certain limitations of traditional auction theory within the context of cryptocurrency.

2. Prediction markets

Prediction markets which have recently seen several decentralized variants, are another example of an area where traditional mechanism design research has a lot to say. Here, the objective might be to specify incentive compatible mechanisms that extract the true beliefs of agents about the probability of different events in order to make accurate predictions. As with auctions, the theory has tools to deal with more sophisticated assumptions, such as situations where agents behave strategically and/or may seek to manipulate the beliefs of other agents in order to alter market prices in their favor. There are also some more awkward problems, such the fact that agents' private information isn't always easily convertible to discrete probabilities.

Second Part

Case Studies

Bitcoin

L et's talk Bitcoin. The bitcoin network is a public, decentralized peer-to-peer payment network that allows users to send and receive native bitcoin tokens without a bank intermediary. Bitcoin, also known as BTC, is the only cryptocurrency trading on the bitcoin network. Furthermore, Bitcoin is the first successful implementation of a distributed cryptocurrency, described in 1998 by Wei Dai on the cypherpunks mailing list.

Let's have a closer look at it to understand what Bitcoin actually is and how it differentiates from other cryptocurrencies. Bitcoin transactions are recorded using a digital ledger, and nodes ensure a so-called Proof-of-Work (PoW) consensus mechanism is followed.

Furthermore, Bitcoin itself is fungible, meaning every bitcoin is alike. A key difference between using Bitcoin instead of your bank account is that transactions are faster, more secure, and cheaper. Pretty amazing, right? Each payment transaction is broadcast to the network and included in the blockchain so that the included bitcoins cannot be spent twice. After around an hour, each transaction is locked in time by the massive amount of processing power that continues to extend the blockchain. Using these techniques, Bitcoin provides a fast and highly reliable payment network that anyone can use.

Furthermore, compared to your local bank, Bitcoin is not controlled by an entity, creating an independent decentralized system. There are a lot of properties that make Bitcoin unique. For one, Bitcoin cannot be printed or debased. Only 21 million bitcoins will ever exist.

> ***Digital or public ledger -*** *A record keeping system that derived its name from the established record-keeping system used to record information, such as agricultural commodity prices and news. The public ledger was available for general public viewing as well as for verification. Blockchain based systems rely on a similar record-keeping and public verification mechanism, which is how the name came about.*
>
> *These ledgers are modern-day record-keeping systems that form the backbone of many cryptocurrencies. The ledger system allows users to anonymously maintain the identities of participants, their respective cryptocurrency balances, and a record of all the transactions executed between them.*

The simplicity of Bitcoin's design is what makes it so beautiful, so let us talk a bit more about it.

As mentioned before, the total supply is 21 million, which is pre-programmed. A block is mined about every 10 minutes, rewarding the miner 6.25 BTC (when Bitcoin started it was 50 BTC per block, then 25, 12.5, 6.25, etc). Every 210K blocks, the reward is halved — with 10 minutes per block that amounts to a halving every 4 years. The next halving will take place around 2024.

Figure 29: Bitcoin halving illustrated

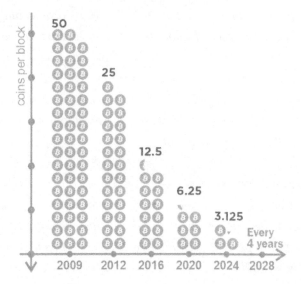

With the ongoing Bitcoin halving we can expect that the final Bitcoin will be mined around the year 2140. The current amount in circulation shows we are already at almost 90% of the total supply, though the last 10% will take a lot longer to mine.

Bitcoin's inflation rate is cut in half every 4 years, and to date, we can see that this has caused a price surge in anticipation of reduced supply - however, it would be foolish to take the past for granted. Instead, we should not assume a constant price increase due to the halving but instead consistently evaluate Bitcoin within the environment it operates in.

Figure 30: Bitcoin tokenomics illustration (simplified)

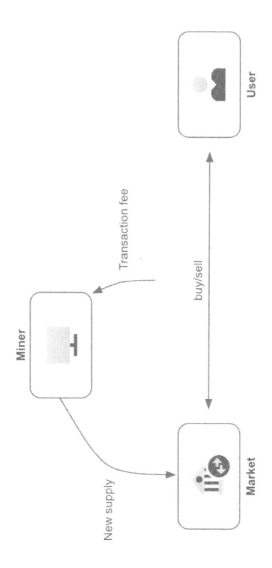

If we want to calculate the total issuance of bitcoin for this year (approximation) we can do it the following way:

$$\frac{Total\ minutes\ per\ year}{10} \times 6.25$$

We first divide the number of minutes in one year by 10, as a block is mined every 10 minutes. In a next step, we multiply this new number by 6.25 (for this year at least) since every block mined issues 6.25 new bitcoin. The total annual new supply is currently around 328 thousand bitcoin.

Bitcoin mining is the process of verifying new transactions to the Bitcoin digital currency system, as well as the process by which new bitcoin enter into circulation. Miners receive the latest batch of transaction data, which is then run through a cryptographic algorithm. A hash (or string of numbers and letters) that does not reveal any transaction data is generated and used for validation purposes. The hash is designed this way to help ensure that its corresponding block has not been tampered with. If even one number is different or out of place, the corresponding data generates a different hash. The previous block's hash is included within the next block so that changes in the previous blocks are reflected in the new generated hash. The hash must also be below a specified target set by the hash algorithm. If the generated hash is too large, it is generated again until it is below its specified target.

The hashing process is designed to make solving transaction-related algorithms more challenging over time. This means solving these algorithms also requires more and more computing resources.

To reward bitcoin miners, a certain number of bitcoins are issued to them in exchange for doing the work. Bitcoin mining, therefore, accomplishes three tasks. It verifies bitcoin transactions, creates a way to issue more currency and incentivizes more bitcoin mining. Keep in mind, due to Bitcoin's more or less lumpy design, only a single user is awarded in each block interval – their chance of getting the award is proportional to the hash rate they've contributed. While this seems counterintuitive at first, it reduces the attack surface significantly. One of the downsides is the higher variance - to have any real chance to win anything at all, you need a significant hash rate, though if you do win, you win big. However, this higher variance is mitigated simply by higher-level mining pools, which have the direct effect of reducing variance.

One of bitcoin's objectives is to maximize the security of the network. We can see the hash rate (compute power) as a way to secure the bitcoin network, making it expensive to roll back changes to the transaction log. In addition, block rewards manifest this objective, by giving bitcoins to people who improve the network's compute power.

That being said, there are only 2.5 million Bitcoin addresses with more than $10 worth of Bitcoin. Despite the widespread attention that Bitcoin has received, the number of people who actually own significant amounts of Bitcoin is relatively small. However, as of April 2023, there are over 100,000 merchants around the world that accept Bitcoin as a form of payment and adoption is rising

Ethereum

The Ethereum network is a public, decentralized peer-to-peer network. Like Bitcoin, it uses nodes and allows users to send and receive cryptocurrency—in this case, Ether.

Nodes - Simply put, a node is a computer connected to other computers which follows a set of rules and shares information. A "full node" is a computer that hosts and synchronizes a copy of the entire blockchain. There are also "light nodes" that depend on full nodes for functioning. They require significantly fewer download and storage capacities than full nodes since they only download block headers from the blockchain and thus do not store the entire blockchain. Their only task is to verify transactions in the blockchain using simplified payment verification (SPV).

Ethereum (*or Mastercoin for those who remember*) was primarily created to deploy decentralized applications (dApps) and smart contracts. Decentralized apps, or dApps, are computer programs that interact with the Ethereum blockchain. Smart contracts are different from dApps. They operate on the Ethereum blockchain and are contracts that automatically execute without an intermediary once certain conditions are met. These contracts can be used to automate a wide range of tasks and transactions, from financial services to supply chain management.

While Bitcoin aims to be a decentralized payment system and a store of value. Ethereum is more than a payment system and allows smart contracts and apps to be built on it, making it a more "*sophisticated*" blockchain.

Ethereum has become one of the most popular blockchain platforms, with a vast ecosystem of developers and users building and using a variety of decentralized applications. The platform has undergone several upgrades since its launch in 2015, with the most recent and significant being the introduction of Ethereum 2.0, which promises to significantly improve the network's scalability and security.

Figure 31: Ethereum tokenomics illustration (simplified)

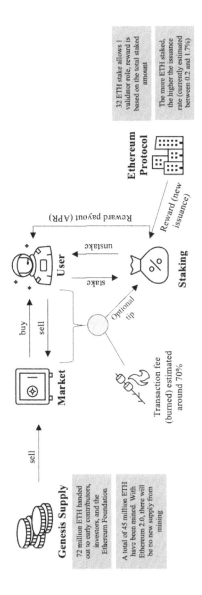

Ethereum initially used a proof-of-work (PoW) consensus mechanism, similar to Bitcoin. As we have seen, PoW requires miners to perform complex mathematical calculations to validate transactions and add them to the blockchain, which consumes a significant amount of computing power and energy.

To address the scalability and energy consumption issues associated with PoW, Ethereum transitioned to a proof-of-stake (PoS) consensus mechanism through a series of upgrades. PoS replaces the energy-intensive mining process with staking, where network participants can lock up their Ether as collateral to validate transactions and earn rewards.

The transition to PoS began with the launch of the Ethereum 2.0 beacon chain in December 2020. The beacon chain is a separate chain that runs in parallel to the existing Ethereum network and serves as a foundation for the full PoS upgrade. The beacon chain allows users to stake their Ether and participate in the network's consensus process.

Under PoS, network participants are called validators, and they are responsible for validating transactions and adding new blocks to the blockchain. Validators are chosen based on the amount of Ether they have staked, with larger stakes increasing the chances of being selected to validate transactions and earn rewards.

In addition to validating transactions, validators are also responsible for attesting to the validity of other validators' blocks. This incentivizes honest behavior and penalizes malicious actors who attempt to manipulate the network. Validators who behave honestly earn rewards, while those who act maliciously lose their staked Ether.

Whoever is willing to stake 32 ETH can become a validator or can take multiple validator roles when the stake is multiplied too. Validators are rewarded by an annual return (APR). This payout is the single source of new network issuance in Ethereum 2.0. The more ETH is staked, the lower the annual return for stakers, as more ETH is issued.

It is important to keep in mind that staking comes with responsibilities: Storing data, processing transactions and adding new blocks. If you fail to validate, go offline or act maliciously, you can be penalized, potentially chewing away your profits.

Token standards

Token standards are the set of rules that allow the development of cryptocurrency tokens on different blockchain protocols. However, before delving into token standards, it is helpful to understand the mechanisms of a smart contract standard.

Fundamentally, smart contract standards are rules that a smart contract must comply with to function as intended on the underlying blockchain network. These standards are application-level specifications, such as token standards, name registries, and library-package formats. With this set of smart contract standards and clearly defined parameters, anyone with sufficient knowledge may create their own ERC token. In short, they enable smart contracts to perform their basic functions.

Ethereum Request for Comment (ERC) is a set of technical documents containing guidelines for developing a smart contract. They define specific functions for each token type and facilitate the interaction between applications and smart contracts. Interestingly, anyone can create an ERC. However, it requires going through the Ethereum Improvement Proposal (EIP) process, which is a document with the proposed features and processes for the Ethereum blockchain network. We will be touching on some key EIPs later in this chapter.

Once a developer submits a proposal, Ethereum's core developers will assess and scrutinize it. Next, the proposal will be accepted, finalized, and implemented if the community deems it an important addition to the blockchain ecosystem. As soon as this process is complete, the initial document becomes an ERC standard for other developers to create their own tokens.

For blockchains that support smart contracts, token standards represent a guide for creating, issuing, and deploying new tokens on the underlying blockchain.

Most blockchain smart contracts currently use Ethereum, with the most common token standards being ERC-20, ERC-721, ERC-777, and ERC-1155. The emergence of new token standards on Ethereum has opened up a range of possibilities for developers to create new types of tokens that can represent different types of assets, such as real estate, art, and commodities. This has the potential to revolutionize how assets are represented and traded, making it easier to fractionalize ownership and facilitate peer-to-peer trading.

ERC-20

ERC-20 is by far the most used token standard on Ethereum. It is the standard for fungible tokens, which are tokens that are interchangeable and have the same value.

Keep in mind, Ethereum is not just a blockchain, like Bitcoin - it is a platform. This means that other tokens can run on top of it, and decentralized applications can be established via smart contracts.

As Ethereum's popularity grew, and people started creating their own smart contracts, a problem arose: How do you get these different contracts to interact with each other? The answer was ERC-20. This is a standard or "set of rules" that make it easier for contracts to interact. ERC-20 was first proposed by Fabian Vogelsteller in 2015 as a way to standardize the creation and deployment of tokens on Ethereum. The proposal was quickly adopted by the Ethereum community and has since become the de facto standard for creating fungible tokens on the platform.

The ERC-20 token standard allows developers to create their own tokens on the Ethereum network. It has provided an easier route for companies to develop blockchain products instead of building their own cryptocurrency. And while some tokens, such as Uniswap's UNI token, have remained ERC-20 tokens; other cryptocurrencies, such as Binance's BNB, have since jumped over to their own blockchains. In April 2019, Binance officially announced the launch of Binance Chain, a new blockchain specifically designed for high-speed trading and decentralized applications. Binance Chain was developed using the Tendermint consensus algorithm

Currently, most ERC-20 tokens on Ethereum are designed to be used to pay for goods and services.

1. **Fungible** - The code of each individual token is the same as any other, though transaction histories can

be used to identify and separate out the tokens involved.

2. Transferable - They can be sent from one address to another.

3. Fixed supply - A fixed number of tokens must be created so that developers cannot issue more tokens and raise the supply.

Since the ERC-20 token standard was finalized, over 500,000 tokens compatible with ERC-20 have been issued. As a matter of fact, ERC-20 tokens have become one of the most popular standards for creating and issuing tokens on the Ethereum blockchain. They have several advantages, making them a popular choice for companies and individuals looking to build decentralized applications and token-based economies.

First, ERC-20 tokens are relatively easy to create and issue, as the standard provides a clear set of guidelines and functions that can be used to build and deploy new tokens. This has helped to democratize the process of building decentralized applications and has enabled a wider range of individuals and companies to participate in the crypto economy.

Another key advantage of ERC-20 tokens is their interoperability. Because ERC-20 tokens are built on the Ethereum blockchain, they can be used across different applications and exchanges that support the standard. This makes it easier for tokens to gain wider adoption and liquidity, as they can be easily traded and used across a variety of platforms.

ERC-20 tokens are also widely accepted by cryptocurrency exchanges, wallets, and other platforms that support the Ethereum network. This makes it easier for users to trade, store, and use ERC-20 tokens, as they can easily be integrated into existing platforms and systems.

In addition, ERC-20 tokens can be transferred at a lower cost than traditional cryptocurrency transfers, as they do not require the same level of processing power as other types of transactions. This makes ERC-20 tokens an attractive option for individuals and companies looking to reduce their transaction costs and improve the efficiency of their operations.

ERC-20 tokens are built on the Ethereum blockchain, which means they can take advantage of smart contract functionality. This allows for more complex and customizable token models, such as tokens with built-in voting or governance mechanisms. This has enabled a wide range of use cases for ERC-20 tokens, from utility tokens to security tokens to governance tokens.

Finally, ERC-20 tokens are decentralized, meaning they are not controlled by a single entity or authority. This makes them more resistant to censorship, hacking, and other attacks. Additionally, because ERC-20 tokens are decentralized, they can be used to create more democratic and transparent systems, such as decentralized exchanges or decentralized autonomous organizations (DAOs).

While ERC-20 tokens have several advantages, they also have some disadvantages that are important to consider. One major issue with ERC-20 tokens is the low throughput and slow transaction speeds of the Ethereum network.

The Ethereum network has faced significant scalability challenges, which led to high transaction fees and slower confirmation times. This can be problematic for ERC-20 tokens, as they are built on top of the Ethereum blockchain and rely on its infrastructure for processing transactions. When the network becomes congested, ERC-20 token transactions can become delayed or even fail altogether, which can be frustrating for users and limit the scalability of ERC-20 token-based projects.

Another potential disadvantage of ERC-20 tokens is the lack of standardization. While the ERC-20 standard provides a clear set of guidelines and functions for building tokens, it does not ensure that all tokens will be created and managed in the same way. This can lead to confusion and potential security risks, as tokens with different standards or management practices may be more vulnerable to attack or misuse.

Finally, ERC-20 tokens are not suitable for all use cases. While they are well-suited for utility tokens and other types of digital assets, they may not be the best option for more complex applications or financial instruments. In particular, security tokens and other types of regulated assets may require more specific standards and regulatory compliance measures that are not provided by the ERC-20 standard.

The future of ERC-20 tokens is closely tied to the development of the Ethereum blockchain and its ecosystem. While ERC-20 tokens have become a popular choice for building decentralized applications and token-based economies, the Ethereum network has faced significant scalability challenges, which have limited the scalability and throughput of ERC-20 tokens.

To address these challenges, the Ethereum community is actively working on several solutions that could improve the performance and scalability of the network. For example, the Ethereum 2.0 upgrade is expected to bring significant improvements to the network's throughput and transaction speeds, which could benefit ERC-20 tokens by making them more efficient and cost-effective to use.

Another potential development for ERC-20 tokens is the emergence of new standards or protocols that could improve their functionality or usability. For example, the ERC-223 standard has been proposed as a more advanced version of the ERC-20 standard, which could offer additional features and functionality for developers building ERC-20 tokens.

Additionally, we may see more use cases for ERC-20 tokens beyond the current applications in digital assets and utility tokens. For example, ERC-20 tokens could be used to represent more traditional financial instruments, such as stocks or bonds, which could be traded and managed in a more decentralized and transparent way using smart contracts and blockchain technology.

ERC-20 tokens are widely used and their traction will continue as long as Ethereum maintains its status. If anything, their biggest threat is from the enemy within new Ethereum standards.

ERC-721

The ERC-721 token standard is a non-fungible token standard that enables developers to create and manage unique digital assets on the Ethereum blockchain. Proposed by William Entriken, Dieter Shirley, Jacob Evans, and Nastassia Sachs in January 2018, ERC-721 has rapidly become one of the most popular token standards on the Ethereum network.

Unlike fungible tokens, which are interchangeable and have the same value, non-fungible tokens are unique and indivisible. ERC-721 provides a standardized framework for building and managing non-fungible tokens on the Ethereum blockchain, enabling new use cases for token-based economies.

One of the key features of ERC-721 is its ability to implement an API for tokens within smart contracts. This allows developers to create and manage digital assets with unique properties and values, which can be used in a variety of applications such as gaming, art, collectibles, and more.

ERC-721 tokens provide a range of functionalities that enable them to be used in a variety of applications. These functionalities include transferring tokens from one account to another, checking the current token balance of an account, identifying the owner of a specific token, and determining the total supply of the token available on the network. Additionally, ERC-721 tokens have other functionalities such as the ability to approve that an amount of token from an account can be moved by a third-party account.

To be called an ERC-721 Non-Fungible Token Contract, a smart contract must implement certain methods and events. Once deployed, the contract is responsible for keeping track of the created tokens on the Ethereum network. This ensures that each token is unique and can be tracked and managed independently.

One of the key benefits of ERC-721 is its ability to enable new use cases for token-based economies. For example, it has enabled the creation of digital art and collectibles, which can be bought and sold on the Ethereum network. It has also enabled new gaming experiences, where players can own unique in-game assets that can be traded and managed like real-world assets.

However, ERC-721 tokens also have some limitations and challenges that should be taken into consideration. For example, they can be more complex to create and manage than fungible tokens, which can require more technical expertise and resources. Additionally, the low throughput and slow transaction speeds of the Ethereum network can limit the scalability of ERC-721-based projects, particularly during periods of high network congestion.

ERC-777

The ERC-777 token standard is a more advanced version of the popular ERC-20 token standard that aims to address some of its limitations. Proposed in August 2017 by Jacques Dafflon, the ERC-777 token standard provides a more efficient mechanism for smart contracts to send and receive tokens, making it an attractive option for developers looking to build advanced token-based economies.

One of the key features of the ERC-777 token standard is the introduction of a new mechanism called Hooks. Hooks is a function that combines what would have been two messages - sending tokens and notifying a contract - into one. This makes the process of sending and receiving tokens more efficient, reducing the overall transaction time and cost.

Another notable feature of the ERC-777 token standard is the ability to reject transactions from blacklisted addresses. This provides an additional layer of security and makes it easier for developers to protect their token ecosystems from malicious actors.

One of the most significant advantages of the ERC-777 token standard is that it remains backwards compatible with the ERC-20 standard, rather than rendering it obsolete. This means that tokens built on the ERC-20 standard can freely interact with tokens built on the ERC-777 standard because both of these standards use the same underlying functions. This allows for a smooth transition for developers looking to migrate from ERC-20 to ERC-777, while also enabling interoperability between different token-based ecosystems.

Overall, the ERC-777 token standard offers several advantages over its predecessor, including improved efficiency, enhanced security, and backwards compatibility with ERC-20. As the Ethereum ecosystem continues to evolve, we can expect to see even more innovative use cases for ERC-777 tokens, particularly in the context of advanced token-based economies and decentralized finance.

ERC-1155

The ERC-1155 token standard is a highly advanced token standard that has been developed to address some of the limitations of its predecessors. This standard provides a range of benefits to developers and users, including greater efficiency, flexibility, and interoperability. The ERC-1155 token standard was developed by Enjin, a leading blockchain development company that specializes in creating decentralized gaming platforms. Enjin developed this standard to address the limitations of previous token standards, specifically the lack of flexibility for batch transfers.

ERC-1155 is designed to manage multiple token types in a single contract, making it incredibly versatile and allowing it to govern an infinite number of tokens. This represents a significant improvement over previous token standards, which were designed for specific use cases and lacked the flexibility to handle multiple asset types.

One of the most notable features of ERC-1155 is its support for batch transfers, which allows multiple assets to be bundled in one smart contract. This significantly reduces the potential for network congestion and lowers transaction costs, making it a more efficient and cost-effective option for developers.

ERC-1155 also offers improved interoperability with other token standards, enabling contracts to be easily integrated with other smart contracts and applications. This is achieved through the use of a standardized interface, which allows for greater compatibility and more seamless interactions with other platforms and protocols.

In addition to these benefits, ERC-1155 offers improved scalability, as it allows multiple assets to be managed under a single contract, reducing the overall contract deployment and maintenance costs. It also offers greater flexibility in the creation of token-based ecosystems, as it can handle both fungible and non-fungible tokens within the same contract.

Moreover, ERC-1155 supports semi-fungible tokens, a new type of token that is unique but can be divided into smaller denominations, making them partially fungible. This provides even greater flexibility and innovation in token-based ecosystems, enabling the creation of tokens with different properties and use cases.

Since its introduction, ERC-1155 has gained significant traction, with many projects adopting this standard for their token-based ecosystems. Some notable examples include Enjin, which developed the standard, and gaming platforms like Decentraland and ChainGuardian.

Overall, the ERC-1155 token standard represents a significant improvement over its predecessors, providing developers and users with greater efficiency, flexibility, scalability, and interoperability. With its ability to manage multiple token types and handle both fungible and non-fungible assets, we can expect to see even more innovative use cases for this token standard in the future.

ERC-998/1400/223

ERC-998 is a token standard that has been developed to improve interoperability between different blockchains. This standard allows for the creation of tokens that can be owned by multiple contracts and moved between different blockchains. This represents a significant development in the blockchain ecosystem, as it enables greater flexibility and interoperability between different applications and platforms.

Interestingly, the development of ERC-998 was inspired by the concept of nested dolls, where a smaller doll is contained within a larger doll. In the context of ERC-998, this concept is applied to the ownership of tokens, allowing for greater complexity and flexibility in the management of tokens across different contracts and blockchains.

Another notable token standard is ERC-1400, which is designed specifically for security tokens. Security tokens are tokens that represent ownership of a particular asset, such as equity in a company or real estate. As such, they require more stringent regulatory compliance and security measures, including know-your-customer (KYC) protocols. ERC-1400 provides the necessary features to enable security tokens to be sold and traded in a compliant and secure manner.

Finally, the ERC-223 token standard is designed to improve the efficiency and cost-effectiveness of token transactions. Currently, fees for transactions on the Ethereum network are paid in Ether, the native cryptocurrency of the platform. ERC-223 allows for transaction fees to be paid in the tokens involved in the transaction, reducing the need for Ether and providing greater flexibility and efficiency for users.

Overall, these token standards represent significant developments in the evolution of blockchain technology, enabling greater interoperability, security, and efficiency for blockchain-based applications. With the continued development and adoption of these standards, we can expect to see even more innovative use cases and applications for blockchain technology in the future.

While token standards like ERC-20, ERC-721, ERC-777, ERC-1155, and ERC-998 have significantly contributed to the growth and development of the Ethereum ecosystem, the Ethereum Improvement Proposals (EIPs) have played an equally important role. These proposals represent a collaborative effort by the Ethereum community to improve and enhance the functionality and performance of the Ethereum network. In the following section, we will explore some of the most significant EIPs that have been proposed and implemented on the Ethereum network.

EIP-1559

Ethereum is one of the most widely used blockchain networks in the world, supporting thousands of decentralized applications and hundreds of thousands of daily transactions. However, as the network became more congested and popular, it struggled with high transaction fees and slow confirmation times. This led to frustration among users and developers, and it became clear that a solution was needed.

Enter EIP-1559, the Ethereum Improvement Proposal that changed the game for gas fees on the Ethereum network. Proposed in 2018 by Ethereum core developer Eric Conner, EIP-1559 aimed to overhaul the way that gas fees were calculated and paid on the network.

Before EIP-1559, Ethereum users had to manually set their own gas fees for each transaction. This created a highly competitive and unpredictable market, where users would have to compete with each other to get their transactions processed as quickly as possible. This resulted in a situation where gas fees could become extremely high during periods of high network congestion, which made using the network prohibitively expensive for many users.

EIP-1559 aimed to solve this problem by introducing a new system for calculating and paying gas fees. The proposal suggested setting a base fee for each block on the Ethereum network, which would be automatically adjusted based on network congestion. This would make gas fees more predictable, stable, and would help prevent users from having to overpay for transactions during periods of high congestion.

In addition to this, EIP-1559 also proposed a new mechanism for burning a portion of the gas fees paid by users. This mechanism would help reduce the overall supply of Ether and would provide additional economic incentives for users to pay reasonable gas fees.

EIP-1559 faced significant opposition and controversy within the Ethereum community, with some users and developers arguing that it would make the network less predictable and could lead to a more centralized system. However, after extensive debate and testing, EIP-1559 was finally included in the London hard fork update in August 2021.

The impact of EIP-1559 was immediately felt on the network. Gas fees became more predictable and stable, and users reported significant cost savings when making transactions. According to some estimates, EIP-1559 reduced the daily cost of securing the Ethereum network by 42%, from $47M to $33M.

EIP-1962

EIP-1962 is an Ethereum Improvement Proposal that proposes to add precompiled contracts for the alt_bn128 elliptic curve, which would provide additional cryptographic functions to the Ethereum network. This EIP was authored by Christian Reitwießner and Vitalik Buterin and was first proposed in February 2018.

The alt_bn128 elliptic curve is a particular curve used in some cryptographic applications, such as zk-SNARKs (Zero-Knowledge Succinct Non-Interactive Argument of Knowledge). zk-SNARKs are a type of zero-knowledge proof that allows one party (the prover) to convince another party (the verifier) of the truth of a statement without revealing any additional information beyond the statement's truthfulness.

Before EIP-1962, Ethereum did not natively support the alt_bn128 curve, and implementing it was challenging due to the limited resources available in the EVM (Ethereum Virtual Machine). However, with the proposal of EIP-1962, precompiled contracts would be added to the Ethereum network that would enable more efficient and secure operations on the alt_bn128 curve.

One of the significant advantages of EIP-1962 is its potential to reduce the cost and complexity of implementing zk-SNARKs on Ethereum. Prior to this EIP, developers needed to perform elliptic curve operations using EVM opcodes or implement their own low-level elliptic curve operations, which can be challenging and resource-intensive.

Furthermore, by introducing precompiled contracts for the alt_bn128 curve, EIP-1962 could enable more advanced cryptographic applications on the Ethereum network, such as anonymous transactions and confidential smart contracts. These applications could have significant implications for the privacy and security of the Ethereum network, and the broader blockchain ecosystem.

EIP-2718

EIP-2718, proposed by Anthony Towns and Tim Ruffing, is a recent Ethereum Improvement Proposal that aims to enhance the flexibility and extensibility of the Ethereum network. This proposal introduces a new type of transaction format that allows for more efficient and secure protocol upgrades, as well as improved interoperability with other blockchains.

The new transaction format proposed by EIP-2718 introduces a field that allows for the identification of a transaction type. This allows for multiple transaction types to be included within a single block, each with its own set of rules and parameters. This added flexibility will enable developers to create new transaction types and functionalities without the need for a hard fork, which is a major change to the underlying protocol that requires a network-wide consensus.

This new proposal builds upon previous work in the Ethereum community to improve network efficiency and scalability. The addition of the transaction type field is a significant step towards making the network more extensible and flexible for developers. The proposal also includes improvements to the signature scheme and the use of domain separation to enhance security.

One of the unique features of EIP-2718 is that it is designed to be backwards compatible with existing transaction formats, such as the current Ethereum Transaction and Contract Creation formats. This means that existing smart contracts and applications will not need to be updated to work with the new transaction format.

In addition to its immediate benefits, EIP-2718 has the potential to pave the way for more sophisticated smart contract functionality in the future. The ability to add new transaction types opens up a wide range of possibilities for the development of complex smart contracts that can perform a variety of functions.

There are a lot more EIPs to learn about and to get the most detailed understanding check out https://eips.ethereum.org/all

Ethereum has become a key player in the world of blockchain technology and cryptocurrency, offering a robust and flexible platform for decentralized applications and smart contracts. The Ethereum ecosystem has given rise to numerous token standards like ERC-20, ERC-721, ERC-777, and ERC-1155, which have expanded the possibilities for creating fungible and non-fungible assets on the blockchain.

In addition, the development of EIPs such as EIP-1559, EIP-1962, and EIP-2718 continues to push the boundaries of what is possible with Ethereum, improving network efficiency, and enabling new use cases.

It is also fascinating to note some unique facts about Ethereum, such as the fact that its original name was not Ethereum, but rather "Mastercoin" or "The Real World Computing Project." Ethereum was not the first blockchain to implement smart contracts, and the Ethereum network has its own programming language, Solidity, which is used to write smart contracts. Moreover, the Ethereum blockchain was designed to be ASIC-resistant, setting it apart from other cryptocurrencies like Bitcoin.

With its innovative approach to blockchain technology and its expanding ecosystem of applications and tools, Ethereum continues to pave the way for the future of decentralized finance and digital assets. The possibilities are endless, and it will be exciting to see what the future holds for Ethereum and the broader blockchain industry.

Uniswap

U niswap is a decentralized exchange (DEX) built on the Ethereum blockchain. It was created by Hayden Adams in 2018 and has quickly become one of the most popular DEXs in the cryptocurrency space.

The concept of Uniswap is based on the Automated Market Maker (AMM) model, which allows users to trade cryptocurrencies without the need for a traditional order book. Instead, trades are executed based on a mathematical formula that automatically sets the price of an asset based on its supply and demand. This model is designed to reduce liquidity issues and improve the user experience by eliminating the need for order matching.

Uniswap's development has been driven by its community, with many contributors making significant contributions to the platform's growth and development. One of the key features of Uniswap is its open-source code, which allows developers to create new applications and tools that can interact with the platform.

Uniswap has gained widespread adoption and has become an important player in the decentralized finance (DeFi) ecosystem. Its trading volumes have surged over the past year, with daily trading volumes frequently surpassing those of some centralized exchanges.

In September 2020, Uniswap launched its native token, UNI, through an airdrop to users who had previously used the platform. The launch of the UNI token was seen as a significant milestone for the project, as it gave users a stake in the platform's governance and incentivized liquidity providers to continue supporting the platform.

Tokenomics

UNI is the native governance token of the Uniswap protocol.

UNI has several key use cases within the Uniswap ecosystem. First, it allows holders to participate in the governance of the protocol by voting on proposals to change the protocol's code or parameters. These proposals can include changes to fees, rewards, and other parameters that impact the operation of the protocol. Holders can submit proposals themselves or delegate their voting power to others.

Second, UNI is used to incentivize liquidity provision on the Uniswap platform. Liquidity providers earn a share of trading fees proportional to the amount of liquidity they provide to a particular Uniswap pool. In addition to these fees, liquidity providers also receive UNI tokens as a reward for their participation in the network. The amount of UNI awarded to liquidity providers varies depending on the pool and the amount of liquidity they provide.

Third, UNI can be used to pay for transaction fees on the Uniswap platform. This is particularly useful for users who want to trade smaller amounts of assets on the platform, as it can be more cost-effective than paying transaction fees in Ether (ETH).

Finally, UNI can be traded on a variety of cryptocurrency exchanges, which can provide liquidity for the token and allow for price discovery.

The total supply of UNI is capped at 1 billion tokens, with approximately 60% of the total supply allocated to community members and the remaining 40% allocated to team members, investors, and advisors. The community allocation includes tokens distributed to liquidity providers, users, and team members.

In terms of token distribution, 15% of the total supply was initially distributed to users who had interacted with the protocol prior to September 1, 2020, with each user receiving 400 UNI tokens. This was followed by an airdrop of 150 million UNI tokens to liquidity providers on Uniswap v1 and v2, which were distributed proportionally based on their liquidity contributions. The remaining 700 million UNI tokens are allocated to team members, investors, and advisors, with vesting periods ranging from 1 to 4 years.

Figure 32: Uniswap tokenomics illustration (simplified)

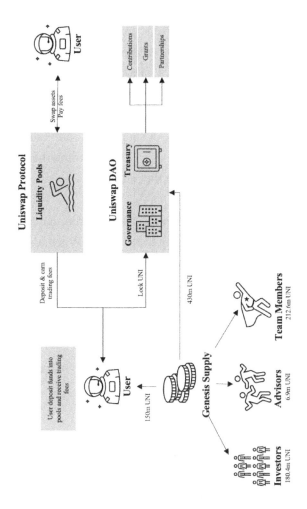

Treasury

The Uniswap decentralized autonomous organization (DAO) treasury is a key component of the Uniswap ecosystem. As a DAO, Uniswap is governed by its community of token holders, who have a say in the development and decision-making processes of the protocol. The Uniswap treasury is where funds are stored and managed, and it plays a crucial role in funding the ongoing development and growth of the protocol.

The Uniswap treasury is funded primarily through a share of the trading fees generated by the protocol. When users make trades on Uniswap, they pay a small fee, which is then split between liquidity providers and the treasury. This fee is currently set at 0.05% per trade, with 0.03% going to liquidity providers and 0.02% going to the treasury. The treasury is managed by the Uniswap DAO, which is made up of UNI token holders who have the power to make decisions regarding the use of funds.

One of the primary uses of the Uniswap treasury is to fund grants for developers and other community members who are contributing to the growth and development of the protocol. The Uniswap Grants program was launched in 2020 and has since provided funding for a wide range of projects, including research and development, user interface design, and community development.

In addition to funding grants, the Uniswap treasury is also used to provide liquidity for new token listings on the protocol. This helps to ensure that new tokens have adequate liquidity when they are first listed, which can help to drive adoption and trading volume.

The Uniswap DAO also has the ability to vote on proposals for other uses of the treasury funds. These proposals may include things like funding additional development or marketing efforts, or even providing liquidity to other DeFi protocols.

One unique aspect of the Uniswap treasury is its transparency. All transactions involving the treasury are publicly viewable on the Ethereum blockchain, which allows for complete transparency and accountability. Additionally, the Uniswap DAO publishes regular updates on the status of the treasury and the use of funds, which helps to keep the community informed and engaged in the governance process.

DAO

The Uniswap DAO is the decentralized autonomous organization that governs the Uniswap protocol. It is a community-driven entity that operates on the Ethereum blockchain and is responsible for making decisions related to the development and direction of Uniswap.

The DAO is structured in a way that allows UNI token holders to participate in the decision-making process. UNI is the governance token of the Uniswap protocol and gives holders the right to vote on proposals submitted to the DAO.

The Uniswap DAO is unique in that it has no formal hierarchy or leaders. Instead, it is designed to operate as a decentralized entity that relies on the collective decision-making of its members. This means that any UNI holder can submit a proposal, and it will be voted on by other UNI holders. This ensures that decision-making power is distributed among the community rather than concentrated in the hands of a few individuals.

The Uniswap DAO uses a quadratic voting system that gives more voting power to those who are more invested in the protocol. This means that UNI holders who have more tokens have more influence over the outcome of a proposal. However, the system also ensures that smaller UNI holders still have a voice and can influence the outcome of a vote.

The governance process of the Uniswap DAO is transparent, and all proposals and votes are publicly visible on the Ethereum blockchain. This ensures that the community can keep track of what is being proposed and voted on and hold the DAO accountable for its decisions.

The Uniswap DAO is responsible for managing the Uniswap treasury, which is used to fund various initiatives related to the development and growth of the protocol. The treasury is funded through various means, including the allocation of a portion of the protocol's trading fees, donations, and grants.

The treasury is managed by a group of individuals known as the Uniswap Grants Committee. The committee is responsible for overseeing the allocation of funds from the treasury and ensuring that they are used in ways that benefit the Uniswap ecosystem.

In addition to managing the treasury, the Uniswap DAO is also responsible for proposing and implementing changes to the protocol. This includes proposing changes to the fee structure, adding new features, and upgrading the protocol to improve its performance and security.

Distribution and Vesting

The distribution of UNI tokens was designed to reward early supporters of the platform and ensure a more equitable distribution of ownership. The initial token distribution consisted of four different groups: users of the protocol, historical liquidity providers, SOCKS NFT redeemers/holders, and team members and investors.

Users of the protocol who had interacted with Uniswap before September 1, 2020, received 400 UNI tokens worth around $1200 at the time of distribution. This was a significant reward for early adopters, and the value of the tokens has since skyrocketed, providing early users with substantial returns.

Historical liquidity providers were also rewarded with UNI tokens based on the amount of liquidity they had provided to the protocol. The rewards were based on a snapshot of liquidity on September 1, 2020, with the total amount of UNI distributed to liquidity providers amounting to 49.2% of the total token supply.

Another group that received UNI tokens were SOCKS NFT redeemers and holders. SOCKS NFTs were a special type of non-fungible token issued by Uniswap Labs, which allowed holders to redeem them for a share of the UNI token allocation.

Lastly, team members and investors received 21.51% of the total UNI token supply, which was vested over a four-year period. The vesting period was designed to align the interests of the team and investors with the long-term success of the protocol.

The distribution of UNI tokens has helped to create a more engaged and committed community around Uniswap, with token holders now having a say in the governance and direction of the protocol. The success of Uniswap and the UNI token has shown that there is a growing demand for decentralized finance (DeFi) protocols and a strong interest in community-led governance models. It will be interesting to see how the UNI token evolves and how the Uniswap community uses it to drive the protocol forward.

The total supply of UNI tokens is 1 billion, with all tokens to be distributed by the end of September 2024. After 4 years of reaching a total of 1 billion UNI tokens, there will be a perpetual inflation rate of 2% per year to ensure continued participation and contribution to Uniswap at the expense of passive UNI holders.

In an airdrop, Uniswap allocated 15% of the total supply, or 150 million tokens, to historical users, including liquidity providers. The remaining 430 million tokens are allocated for distribution to the community through various programs such as contributor grants, community initiatives, liquidity mining, and other initiatives.

The UNI token distribution will be ongoing, with a yearly vesting schedule outlined in a table. The vesting schedule specifies the amount of tokens to be released each year until the total supply is distributed.

In addition to the airdrop and ongoing distribution, Uniswap launched an initial mining program that lasted for two months after the release of UNI tokens. The mining program was available in the ETH/USDT, ETH/USDC, ETH/DAI, and ETH/WBTC pools, with 5 million UNI allocated per pool, for a total of 20 million UNI.

Demand Drivers

One of the key drivers of demand for the UNI token is its utility as a governance token. UNI holders have the power to vote on proposals that impact the future direction of the Uniswap protocol, including the deployment of the protocol on other chains, grant funding, fee tiers, and proposal submission thresholds. However, in order to participate in off-chain governance discussions, token holders must own a minimum of 1,000 UNI. For a formal on-chain proposal, 2.5 million UNI must be staked.

While holding UNI tokens does not currently allocate a portion of the fee revenue generated by liquidity mining to the token holder or to the Uniswap treasury, there is potential for the introduction of a fee-sharing mechanism in the future. This would create added demand for investors to buy and hold UNI tokens, potentially leading to a shortage and driving up the price. However, this has been pointed out for a long time already with no actions being taken so far.

In addition to its governance utility, Uniswap's value is derived from its long-standing history as one of the first and most reputable decentralized exchanges, which has led to a significant first-mover advantage. The Uniswap team has continuously improved and developed the platform, with the upcoming launch of V3 being one of the most highly anticipated updates in the DeFi space.

Another factor that could contribute to increased demand for UNI tokens is the potential for increased adoption and usage of Uniswap. As more users and projects use the platform for trading and liquidity provision, the demand for UNI tokens as a means of participating in governance and accessing certain features of the platform could increase.

Closing Thoughts

Uniswap has undoubtedly made its mark as one of the most impressive decentralized exchanges to date. With its unique features such as low slippage and market fees, Uniswap has gained a competitive advantage and even surpassed the liquidity of some centralized exchanges. As DeFi continues to grow, Uniswap has the potential to become even more valuable by expanding its products to other chains, Layer 2's, and supporting swaps/pools for more tokens.

However, it is important to note that Uniswap's only sustainable inflow to the treasury was the token allocation at genesis. Without adding more utility to the token, Uniswap may struggle during market downturns. Therefore, it is crucial for Uniswap to consider implementing mechanisms that create added demand for investors to buy and hold UNI tokens.

Future use-case for Uniswap include integrating with traditional financial markets. Uniswap already supports tokenized assets, which could be used to represent traditional assets like stocks or commodities. This could allow for seamless trading between crypto assets and traditional assets, opening up new markets and investment opportunities. Additionally, Uniswap's decentralized and transparent nature could make it an attractive platform for asset issuers and traders looking for greater trust and security in their transactions.

Overall, Uniswap sets a great example of how decentralization can lead to success. By continuously developing and improving its protocol, Uniswap has solidified its place in the DeFi ecosystem. As DeFi becomes more mainstream, Uniswap's influence and importance are likely to grow.

MakerDAO

M akerDAO is a permissionless, multi asset, overcollateralized lending platform built on the Ethereum blockchain that facilitates the creation of a stablecoin called Dai. MakerDAO was founded in 2014 by Rune Christensen, and it was one of the earliest projects to offer decentralized lending and borrowing services. The project was initially funded through a crowd sale of its MKR tokens in December 2017, raising over $12 million. In December 2019, MakerDAO launched its second iteration, called Multi-Collateral Dai (MCD), which allowed for the creation of DAI stablecoins backed by collateral other than ETH, such as BAT or USDC.

Dai is a cryptocurrency pegged to the value of the U.S. dollar, with its value maintained through a system of smart contracts and collateralized debt positions (CDPs). The creation of Dai provides a decentralized and transparent alternative to traditional stablecoins that are often backed by fiat currency reserves held by centralized entities.

CDPs, or Collateralized Debt Positions, are an essential component of the MakerDAO system. They allow users to lock up their crypto assets, such as Ethereum, and generate a stablecoin called Dai. CDPs operate by locking up collateral in a smart contract and issuing Dai in return. The amount of Dai that can be generated is dependent on the value of the collateral and the collateralization ratio, which is the ratio of the value of the collateral to the value of the Dai generated. For example, if a user locks up $200 worth of Ethereum with a collateralization ratio of 150%, they can generate up to $133 worth of Dai. The collateralization ratio acts as a safeguard against market volatility and ensures that the value of the collateral remains higher than the value of the Dai generated. CDPs can be managed by the user and closed at any time by paying back the generated Dai plus a stability fee, which is a small interest rate charged for using Dai.

MakerDAO operates through two tokens: MKR and DAI. MKR is a governance token that enables token holders to vote on proposals related to the MakerDAO system, including adjusting collateral requirements and stability fees. DAI, on the other hand, is a stablecoin that can be used for payments, trading, and lending, among other use cases.

In order to create Dai, users must first deposit collateral in the form of Ethereum (ETH) into a CDP. They can then generate Dai against the collateral by locking up a certain amount of ETH, which serves as collateral for the newly created Dai. The value of the collateralized ETH is monitored in real-time and the CDP is automatically liquidated if the value of the collateral falls below a certain threshold. This ensures the stability of the Dai pegged to the U.S. dollar.

The MakerDAO system also allows for the adjustment of collateralization ratios and stability fees based on supply and demand of Dai in order to maintain its peg to the U.S. dollar. Through this system, MakerDAO provides a decentralized and transparent alternative to traditional financial systems, offering greater financial access and stability to individuals and businesses around the world.

Tokenomics

MakerDAO's tokenomics is a complex and multifaceted system that underpins the entire platform. The native token of the MakerDAO ecosystem is called MKR, and it is used to govern the platform and provide stability to the Dai stablecoin. MKR is a deflationary ERC-20 token that is burned whenever a CDP is closed with Dai. This creates a unique feedback mechanism that helps to maintain the stability of the Dai peg.

MKR holders have several important roles within the MakerDAO ecosystem. Firstly, they act as governance participants, with the ability to vote on key platform decisions such as changes to the collateral portfolio, changes to the stability fee, and changes to the oracle feeds. MKR holders are also responsible for maintaining the stability of the Dai stablecoin, and they do this by participating in emergency shutdowns, auctioning off collateral in the event of a CDP liquidation, and setting the stability fee.

The stability fee is a key aspect of MakerDAO's tokenomics, and it is charged on all outstanding Dai loans. The stability fee is set by MKR holders, and it acts as a tool to balance the supply and demand of Dai. If demand for Dai is high, the stability fee will increase, which will encourage users to close their CDPs and sell their Dai. Conversely, if demand for Dai is low, the stability fee will decrease, which will encourage users to open CDPs and mint new Dai.

One unique aspect of MakerDAO's tokenomics is the concept of the "MKR burn". As mentioned earlier, MKR is burned whenever a CDP is closed with Dai. This mechanism is designed to ensure that there is always a sufficient amount of collateral backing Dai, which helps to maintain the stability of the stablecoin. Additionally, when MKR is burned, it reduces the total supply of MKR, which can help to increase the value of the remaining tokens. Let's have a closer look at a few elements to understand the MakerDAO tokenomics better.

1. Dai Lending

DAI lending is a key feature of the MakerDAO protocol, which allows users to borrow Maker's decentralized stablecoin, DAI, by depositing collateral. This is achieved through Vaults, which were previously known as Collateralized Debt Positions (CDPs). When a user opens a Vault, they can lock up collateral in the form of approved cryptocurrencies such as ETH, BAT, or USDC, and generate DAI tokens as a loan against that collateral. The amount of DAI a user can borrow depends on the value of the collateral they deposit and the collateralization ratio they choose.

To ensure the stability of the DAI stablecoin, Vault owners are required to pay a Stability Fee, which is a variable-rate fee continuously added to their generated DAI balance. This fee is similar to the interest paid on a traditional bank loan and is designed to incentivize Vault owners to repay their debt in a timely manner. The Stability Fee parameter has a lower bound of 0%, and it can be set and adjusted by MKR token holders through governance voting. The fee is continuously compounded per second, so if the Stability Fee is set to 2%, it will accumulate at 1.000000000627937192491029810 9948% per second.

In addition to the Stability Fee, there is also a Liquidation Penalty that Vault owners must pay if the value of their collateral reaches the Vault's Liquidation Price. This is in addition to the Stability Fees that are charged for their loan position. Liquidation fees historically have been in the 13–16% range, which serves as a powerful incentive for Vault owners to maintain a safe collateralization ratio and repay their loans promptly.

To encourage DAI savings and provide a way for DAI holders to earn interest on their holdings, the MakerDAO protocol offers the DAI Savings Rate (DSR). The DSR allows any DAI holder to earn savings automatically by locking their DAI into the DSR contract in the Maker Protocol. Similar to how one would earn interest by depositing money in a traditional bank, DAI holders can earn interest by locking their DAI in the DSR contract. The DSR is also set and adjusted by MKR token holders through governance voting.

One of the key utilities of the MKR token is its role in MakerDAO governance. MKR token holders are able to stake their tokens in order to vote on proposed changes to the Maker Protocol, as well as ensure the efficiency, transparency, and stability of DAI. MKR holders can also participate in the governance of other aspects of the protocol, such as setting the Stability Fee, managing the DSR, and managing the collateralization ratio. The ability to influence the protocol's governance through MKR staking is a crucial aspect of the DAI lending system.

2. Action System

To understand the full utility of MKR we should also explore Maker DAO's auctions system. Essentially there are three actions we should know about. Surplus, collateral, and debt auctions.

Surplus Auctions

Surplus auctions are triggered when the total amount of stability fees generated by Vaults exceeds the system's expenses, creating a surplus. This surplus is then auctioned off on a decentralized exchange (DEX) to external actors, who use DAI to bid on the surplus. The Maker system takes this DAI and uses it to buy MKR through smart contracts, which is then burned. This reduces the amount of MKR in circulation, effectively removing it from the ecosystem and increasing the value of existing MKR tokens.

The purpose of surplus auctions is to provide a mechanism for MKR token burn, which helps to maintain the value of MKR and stabilize the MakerDAO ecosystem. By removing MKR tokens from circulation, surplus auctions help to reduce the potential for dilution of existing MKR holders' stakes, which in turn can increase the value of the remaining tokens.

Collateral Auctions

Collateral auctions are triggered when a Vault's collateral value falls below the liquidation point, which is the point at which the collateral value can no longer cover the value of the outstanding debt plus the liquidation penalty. In such cases, the protocol seizes the collateral and sells it in a collateral auction, returning the principal, stability fees plus the liquidation penalty to the borrower. The leftover collateral is then sold on a DEX to external actors in exchange for DAI.

The purpose of collateral auctions is to provide a mechanism for liquidation of under-collateralized positions, which helps to maintain the solvency of the MakerDAO ecosystem. By selling the seized collateral on a DEX, the protocol is able to quickly convert the collateral to DAI, which can then be used to cover the outstanding debt plus fees.

Debt Auctions

Debt auctions are triggered when the value of the collateral falls to a point where it can no longer cover the protocol debt plus fees. This can happen when the collateral price drops sharply or no one wants to buy the collateral. In such cases, the protocol initiates a debt auction, whereby the winning bidder pays DAI to cover the outstanding debt and receives newly minted MKR tokens in return.

The purpose of debt auctions is to provide a mechanism for the system to recapitalize itself in the event of under-collateralized positions. By issuing new MKR tokens and selling them for DAI, the system is able to raise the necessary funds to cover the outstanding debt plus fees.

In summary, the different auctions are the main processes through which MKR and DAI are minted and burned. Surplus Auction and Collateral Auction burn DAI, Debt Auctions mint DAI.

3. Relationship between DAI and MKR

MakerDAO is an innovative lending platform that provides users with a decentralized stablecoin, DAI. The value of DAI is pegged to the US dollar and is maintained through a complex system of overcollateralization and automated actions. The relationship between DAI and MakerDAO is fundamental to understanding how the platform operates.

The MakerDAO ecosystem is fueled by the governance token, MKR, which is used to vote on proposals and make decisions about the direction of the platform. MKR is also used to cover system-wide losses and maintain the stability of DAI. In other words, MKR is the backstop for the MakerDAO system.

One of the primary ways that MKR is used to support the MakerDAO ecosystem is through the generation of stability fees. These fees are generated by borrowers who use their collateral to generate DAI. The fees are paid in DAI and are collected by the MakerDAO system. These fees are then used to buy back and burn MKR tokens, thereby reducing the total supply of MKR in circulation.

The relationship between DAI and MKR is mutually beneficial. The stability of DAI is dependent on the health of the MakerDAO ecosystem, which in turn is supported by the demand for and use of DAI. When the demand for DAI increases, so does the demand for MKR, which increases the value of MKR tokens.

However, there are risks associated with the MakerDAO ecosystem. If the system becomes undercollateralized due to poor lending decisions or unforeseen circumstances, new MKR tokens may need to be minted to cover the losses. This can lead to an increase in the supply of MKR tokens, which can lead to a depreciation in the value of MKR.

Overall, the relationship between DAI and MakerDAO is complex. The intertwined nature means that the success of one is dependent on the success of the other, and both are reliant on the support and participation of the wider community. Through a combination of innovative technology and effective governance, MakerDAO has created a powerful and resilient lending platform that has the potential to revolutionize the financial industry

4. The DAI/Dollar peg

Maintaining the peg of DAI to the US dollar is a crucial aspect of the MakerDAO system. To ensure that DAI remains stable, the MakerDAO protocol employs two main strategies: using the DAI Savings Rate (DSR) and the Peg Stability Module (PSM).

Strategy 1 – Dai Savings Rate

Strategy 1 involves using the DAI Savings Rate (DSR) to adjust the attractiveness of borrowing DAI and thus control its liquidity in the market. The DSR is an interest rate paid out to DAI holders who lock their DAI in the DSR contract. By adjusting the DSR, MKR holders can influence the demand for DAI, and thus the market price of DAI.

If the market price of DAI is above $1, indicating that there is too much DAI in circulation, MKR holders can vote to gradually decrease the DSR. This will make it less attractive to hold DAI and more attractive to hold other assets that offer higher returns. This decrease in demand for DAI should help bring the price of DAI back towards $1.

On the other hand, if the market price of DAI is below $1, indicating that there is not enough DAI in circulation, MKR holders can vote to gradually increase the DSR. This will make it more attractive to hold DAI and less attractive to hold other assets. This increase in demand for DAI should help bring the price of DAI back towards $1.

It's important to note that adjusting the DSR is not a panacea for maintaining the DAI peg. The DSR can only influence demand for DAI to a certain extent, and there are other factors at play in the market that can affect the price of DAI. However, it is a useful tool in the toolkit of the MakerDAO community for helping to maintain the stability of DAI.

Strategy 2 - Peg Stability Module

The Peg Stability Module (PSM) is another tool used by MakerDAO to maintain the DAI peg to the US dollar. The PSM allows users to swap collateral for DAI without having to borrow against their collateral. Instead, they can swap it for stablecoins like USDC. The PSM operates similarly to a regular MakerDAO vault, but with a few key differences. First, it has a liquidation ratio of 100%, meaning that there is no risk of liquidation. Second, it has a stability fee set to 0%, which means that there is no interest charged on the DAI generated through the PSM. The PSM is designed to be used during short-term periods of high demand for DAI when the supply is low.

Using the PSM, users can swap their stablecoins for DAI at a fixed rate, effectively creating a price floor for DAI. This can help stabilize the price of DAI and prevent it from dropping too far below the peg. However, the PSM has its limits, and it is not a long-term solution for maintaining the DAI peg. The PSM is only intended to be used during short-term periods of high demand for DAI when the supply is low. In the long term, the MakerDAO system is designed to adjust the supply and demand of DAI using interest rate adjustments.

In addition to maintaining the peg, the PSM also generates revenue for the MakerDAO system. When users swap their stablecoins for DAI through the PSM, they pay a small fee, which generates revenue for the protocol. This fee is lower than the stability fee charged on traditional MakerDAO vaults, but it still provides a source of revenue for the system.

Overall, the combination of Strategy 1 and Strategy 2 allows MakerDAO to maintain the stability of DAI and ensure that it remains pegged to the US dollar. By adjusting the DSR and utilizing the PSM, the system can manage the supply and demand of DAI and stabilize its price. Additionally, the revenue generated by lending income, liquidation income, and trading fees provides a source of income for the MakerDAO system and helps ensure its long-term sustainability.

5. Real World Assets (RWA)

Of the multiple initiatives the community took to increase DAI adoption, the most notable one was onboarding more real world assets (RWA) as collateral. What that means is that Maker now accept RWA as collateral in addition to the approved Crypto based collateral list.

Crypto RWA (Real World Assets) is an emerging concept in the blockchain and cryptocurrency space that seeks to bridge the gap between the traditional financial world and the decentralized digital economy. Essentially, Crypto RWA is a new type of digital asset that is backed by tangible, real-world assets such as real estate, commodities, or other physical assets, and is represented on the blockchain. This innovation has the potential to unlock a vast array of new opportunities for individuals and businesses alike, particularly in areas such as global commerce, investing, and finance.

The idea of Crypto RWA is to bring the benefits of blockchain technology, such as transparency, security, and immutability, to traditional asset-backed instruments, which have traditionally been opaque and difficult to

> *transfer. By using blockchain technology, Crypto RWA can enable a much more efficient and transparent way of managing assets and transactions, which can lead to significant cost savings and other benefits.*
>
> *Some of the key advantages of Crypto RWA include increased liquidity, lower transaction costs, faster settlement times, and enhanced transparency. This could make it easier for investors to participate in traditionally illiquid markets, such as real estate, and could also make it easier for businesses to access funding from a wider pool of investors. Additionally, Crypto RWA can help to reduce the risk of fraud and counterfeiting, as all transactions are recorded on the blockchain, which is a public ledger that is virtually impossible to tamper with.*

By adding RWA as a collateral, Maker increases the types of collateral against which DAI can be borrowed on the platform.

MakerDAO, the decentralized lending protocol that enables the issuance of the stablecoin DAI, has expanded its offering to include real-world assets (RWA) as collateral for DAI loans. This represents a significant step forward in the evolution of decentralized finance (DeFi), as it enables the creation of a bridge between the traditional financial system and the world of blockchain and cryptocurrencies.

Real-world assets are assets that exist outside of the blockchain ecosystem, such as real estate, cars, and other physical assets. By allowing RWA to be used as collateral for DAI loans, MakerDAO opens up a whole new world of possibilities for DeFi. This development has the potential to increase the liquidity and accessibility of the traditional assets market, while also opening up new investment opportunities for crypto investors.

One of the most prominent examples of MakerDAO's expansion into RWA is the partnership between MakerDAO and New Silver, a U.S.-based real estate lending company. New Silver is using the MakerDAO protocol to tokenize their loans and allow investors to invest in their loans through the blockchain. This means that investors can earn interest on their investments while also benefiting from the stability of the DAI stablecoin.

Another example is the partnership between MakerDAO and Centrifuge, a platform that enables the tokenization of real-world assets. Through this partnership, Centrifuge is using the MakerDAO protocol to allow its users to borrow DAI against the value of their real-world assets, such as invoices and receivables. This enables users to access liquidity without having to sell their assets, which can be a major advantage for businesses that need cash flow but don't want to lose their assets.

In terms of numbers, MakerDAO's expansion into RWA has been growing steadily. At the time of writing, there are over $70 million worth of real-world assets being used as collateral on the MakerDAO platform. This represents a significant increase from just a few months ago, when the amount was closer to $20 million. As more partnerships are formed and more assets are added to the platform, this number is expected to continue to grow.

In addition to the benefits for investors and businesses, MakerDAO's expansion into RWA also has the potential to bring more stability and security to the DeFi ecosystem. By providing a bridge between the traditional financial system and the world of blockchain and cryptocurrencies, MakerDAO is helping to create a more integrated and stable financial ecosystem. This could help to attract more institutional investors and bring more mainstream adoption to the world of DeFi.

Overall, MakerDAO's expansion into RWA represents a major step forward for the world of decentralized finance. By enabling the use of real-world assets as collateral for DAI loans, MakerDAO is opening up a whole new world of investment opportunities for both crypto investors and traditional investors. As this trend continues to grow, it has the potential to bring more stability and security to the DeFi ecosystem and help to bring more mainstream adoption to the world of blockchain and cryptocurrencies.

Conclusion

MakerDAO's overcollateralization approach has many benefits. First, it ensures that the DAI remains stable, even in volatile market conditions. Additionally, it provides users with a decentralized lending platform that does not require intermediaries like banks. MakerDAO has already been used in many different applications, such as providing liquidity to decentralized exchanges and offering loans to individuals and businesses.

Looking to the future, the concept of overcollateralized stablecoins like DAI is expected to expand even further. Many believe that these stablecoins have the potential to become a significant part of the global financial system, providing stability and accessibility to financial services for people all over the world.

To further expand its reach, MakerDAO has recently made efforts to expand into real-world assets (RWA), such as real estate and infrastructure projects. This approach has the potential to bring more stability to the DAI ecosystem and further increase its use cases. Some examples of RWA-backed stablecoins include Centrifuge and Harbor Trade Credit.

Looking forward, MakerDAO and other overcollateralized stablecoins are likely to continue expanding their reach and applications, bringing more stability and accessibility to the world of decentralized finance (DeFi).

However, it is important to note that there are risks associated with these assets, including potential regulatory challenges and market volatility. As with any investment, it is important for individuals to do their own research and understand the risks involved before participating in the ecosystem.

There are other risks associated with crypto-backed RWA. One of the main concerns is the potential for over-collateralization, where the value of the collateral exceeds the value of the loan. This can limit the amount of capital that can be deployed and reduce the efficiency of the lending system. In addition, there is also the risk of smart contract vulnerabilities and the potential for hacking or theft.

Curve

C urve is a decentralized exchange (DEX) that is specifically designed for stablecoins and low-volatility assets. The platform is built on the Ethereum blockchain and was launched in January 2020 by a team of experienced blockchain developers. The main goal of Curve is to provide users with an efficient and secure way to trade stablecoins without the high fees and slippage that are often associated with traditional exchanges.

At its core, Curve is an automated market maker (AMM) that uses a constant product market maker algorithm to determine the price of assets. This algorithm is similar to the one used by Uniswap, but it is specifically designed for stablecoins and other low-volatility assets. Instead of relying on order books like traditional exchanges, Curve uses a pool of liquidity that is provided by users who deposit assets into the pool in exchange for liquidity provider (LP) tokens. These

LP tokens represent a share of the liquidity pool, and they can be used to earn trading fees.

The history of Curve is relatively short, but it has already made a significant impact in the world of decentralized finance (DeFi). The platform was launched in January 2020, and it quickly gained popularity among users who were looking for a more efficient and secure way to trade stablecoins. Since then, Curve has continued to grow in popularity, and it is now one of the most widely used DEXs in the DeFi ecosystem.

One of the key benefits of Curve is its focus on stablecoins. Stablecoins are a type of cryptocurrency that is designed to maintain a stable value, usually by pegging their value to a fiat currency like the US dollar. By focusing on stablecoins, Curve is able to provide users with a high degree of price stability and predictability, which is particularly important in a volatile market like cryptocurrency.

Another key benefit of Curve is its low fees. Because Curve uses an AMM instead of an order book, the fees are generally much lower than those charged by traditional exchanges. This makes it an attractive option for users who are looking to trade stablecoins without incurring high fees.

In terms of use cases, Curve is primarily used for trading stablecoins and other low-volatility assets. However, the platform has also been used for other purposes, such as providing liquidity to other DeFi protocols. For example, Curve was used to provide liquidity to the Compound protocol during the "yield farming" craze of 2020, which helped to drive up the demand for Curve's LP tokens.

Tokenomics

Curve Finance's token, CRV, is an ERC-20 standard token that functions as a governance token for the protocol. Holders of CRV have the ability to submit proposals and potential changes to the allocations of pools. The amount of voting power a user has is determined by both the amount of CRV tokens they stake and the amount of time they stake it. This creates a time-weighted voting mechanism that incentivizes long-term holders and investors to participate in the governance process. Additionally, CRV has a value capture mechanism that promotes certain pools, meaning that liquidity providers in certain pools may receive higher rewards than others based on community consensus.

Curve Finance incentivizes users to lock their CRV tokens within the protocol in return for veCRV tokens, which are used for voting on gauge weights. Those who lock CRV tokens are entitled to fees generated by the protocol's liquidity pools. The voting pomp of users is increased by locking their tokens for a longer period of time, with users who have staked more tokens or for a longer period of time possessing greater voting rights.

Currently, a user needs 2500 veCRV tokens (the equivalent of 10,000 CRV locked for a year) to create a new vote. This voting boost serves as an incentive for users to invest themselves in the future of the Curve DAO. Vote locking also increases one's CRV liquidity providing rewards.

Curve Finance launched their CRV token in August 2020, with a total supply of 3.03 billion tokens. The initial supply of 1.3 billion tokens was distributed as follows: 5% to pre-CRV liquidity providers (with a 1-year vesting period), 30% to the Curve team and investors, 3% to employees (with a 2-year vesting period), and 5% to the community reserve. The fully diluted 3.03 billion in supply will be distributed as follows: 62% goes to liquidity providers, 30% to the team and investors (with 2-4 year vesting periods), 3% to employees (with a 2-year vesting period), and 5% to the community reserve.

The distribution schedule is meant to slowly shift voting power from the Curve team and investors to liquidity providers. The supply will not be fully diluted until around the year 2320, with the remaining supply being issued at a decreasing weight of 2.25 per year. This incentivizes long-term participation in the Curve DAO and promotes stability in the protocol's governance.

Overall, Curve's tokenomics incentivizes long-term participation and investment in the protocol's governance while promoting stability and growth. The community-driven governance model allows for consensus-based decision-making and encourages users to actively participate in the future direction of the protocol. As the decentralized finance ecosystem continues to grow and mature, it is likely that Curve Finance will play an important role in the provision of stablecoin liquidity and the development of new financial products.

Convex

Curve and Convex are two interrelated protocols in the decentralized finance ecosystem. While Curve is a decentralized exchange protocol that specializes in stablecoin trading, Convex is a yield optimization platform that is built on top of the Curve protocol. The relationship between the two is symbiotic in nature, as Convex relies on Curve for liquidity and Curve benefits from the increased usage and demand for its platform.

Convex is specifically designed to optimize yields for Curve liquidity providers. It does so by introducing additional incentives and rewards for users who stake their Curve LP tokens on the Convex platform. Users who stake their tokens on Convex receive additional CRV rewards, which are distributed based on the amount of time and quantity of tokens staked. The platform also offers a variety of other incentives, such as boosting the rewards earned from Curve's liquidity pools and providing additional token rewards for LP providers.

The integration between Curve and Convex has been highly successful, with Convex quickly becoming one of the largest stakeholders of Curve LP tokens. This has provided a significant amount of liquidity for Curve, making it more attractive for traders and investors. Additionally, the incentives provided by Convex have helped to incentivize more liquidity providers to join the Curve platform, further increasing its liquidity and trading volume.

Conclusion

Looking forward, Curve is well-positioned to continue growing and expanding its user base. The platform has already proven to be a popular option for users who are looking to trade stablecoins, and it is likely that this trend will continue as more users become aware of the benefits of stablecoins and decentralized exchanges. Additionally, Curve has recently announced plans to expand its offerings to include other assets, such as tokenized stocks and commodities, which could help to further increase its user base and solidify its position as a leading DEX in the DeFi ecosystem.

AAVE

AVE is a decentralized lending platform built on the Ethereum blockchain. It allows users to borrow and lend cryptocurrency assets in a permissionless and trustless manner. AAVE operates as a smart contract that automates the lending process and eliminates the need for intermediaries. The protocol is governed by its native token, AAVE, which enables holders to participate in the governance of the platform. In this chapter, we will delve into the details of AAVE's protocol, its history, and how it works.

AAVE was launched in 2017 under the name ETHLend, which was rebranded to AAVE in 2018. The platform was designed to allow users to borrow and lend Ethereum-based tokens using smart contracts. AAVE quickly gained popularity in the DeFi space, and by 2020, it had become one of the most widely used decentralized lending platforms. In

January 2021, AAVE v2 was launched, which introduced several new features, including flash loans, credit delegation, and gas optimizations.

The lending process on AAVE starts when a user deposits their cryptocurrency into a liquidity pool on the platform. Once deposited, the user can then borrow another cryptocurrency, using their deposited funds as collateral. The amount of cryptocurrency that can be borrowed depends on the value of the collateral deposited and the loan-to-value (LTV) ratio set by the platform. If the value of the collateral falls below a certain threshold, the loan is liquidated, and the collateral is used to repay the borrowed funds.

One of the key features of the AAVE protocol is the ability for users to earn interest on their deposited funds. The interest rate is dynamic and is determined by the supply and demand for each cryptocurrency in the liquidity pool. This means that the interest rate can change over time as market conditions shift. The interest earned by lenders is paid out in the same cryptocurrency that was deposited.

Another feature of the AAVE protocol is the ability for users to take out flash loans. Flash loans are a type of uncollateralized loan that allows users to borrow funds without any collateral, as long as the borrowed funds are returned within the same transaction block. Flash loans are useful for a variety of purposes, such as arbitrage, collateral swaps, and other trading strategies.

The AAVE protocol also offers a governance system that allows AAVE token holders to vote on changes to the platform. AAVE is the native cryptocurrency of the AAVE platform and is used for governance, staking, and fee reduction. AAVE holders can participate in the governance process by submitting and voting on proposals, and staking their tokens to increase their voting power.

The security of the AAVE protocol is maintained through a system of smart contracts that are audited by third-party security firms. The smart contracts are designed to be transparent and tamper-proof, ensuring that all transactions on the platform are secure and verified.

Let us look at a few other elements that AAVE is well-known for.

1. Flash Loans

AAVE's flash loans are a unique feature that allows users to borrow funds without any collateral as long as they can return the funds within the same transaction block. This means that the borrowed funds need to be returned to the AAVE protocol before the transaction is confirmed on the blockchain. If the borrower fails to return the borrowed funds, the entire transaction is reverted, and the loan is canceled. This allows users to take advantage of arbitrage opportunities or execute complex trading strategies without the need for upfront capital.

Flash loans are made possible due to the composability of Ethereum smart contracts. The AAVE protocol uses a specific type of smart contract known as a "receiver" contract, which is an important piece of the flash loan mechanism. The receiver contract acts as a temporary custodian for the borrowed funds and executes specific actions according to the borrower's instructions. Once the actions are completed, the receiver contract returns the borrowed funds to the AAVE protocol, along with any accrued interest.

Flash loans have been a game-changer for the DeFi ecosystem, allowing users to access liquidity without collateral and execute trades that were previously impossible. However, they have also been the target of hacks and exploits due to the lack of collateral. As a result, the AAVE protocol has implemented several measures to prevent flash loan attacks, such as limiting the amount of flash loans per transaction and imposing fees on flash loans.

2. Rate Switching

Rate switching is a unique feature of the AAVE protocol that allows borrowers to switch between fixed and variable interest rates on their loans. This provides users with more flexibility and control over their borrowing costs, allowing them to take advantage of market conditions and adjust their interest rates accordingly.

When a borrower takes out a loan on the AAVE protocol, they can choose between fixed and variable interest rates. Fixed interest rates provide borrowers with a predictable borrowing cost over the loan's duration, while variable interest rates fluctuate based on market conditions. If market interest rates increase, borrowers with variable interest rates will see their borrowing costs rise, while those with fixed interest rates will not be affected.

Rate switching allows borrowers to switch between fixed and variable interest rates at any time during the loan's duration. This means that if a borrower initially chooses a fixed interest rate but market conditions change, they can switch to a variable interest rate to take advantage of lower borrowing costs. Similarly, if a borrower initially chooses a variable interest rate but market conditions become unfavorable, they can switch to a fixed interest rate to protect themselves from rising borrowing costs.

3. Credit Delegation

Credit delegation is a feature of the AAVE protocol that allows users to delegate their borrowing capacity to other users without the need for collateral. This means that users can lend their borrowing capacity to trusted parties, such as family members, friends, or business partners, without the need for collateral or the risk of default.

Credit delegation is made possible by using a smart contract known as a "delegation contract." The delegation contract allows a user to delegate their borrowing capacity to another user, who can then use it to take out loans on the AAVE protocol. The delegator retains control over their borrowing capacity and can revoke the delegation at any time.

Credit delegation has several benefits, including increased access to credit for borrowers and reduced risk for lenders. Borrowers can access credit without the need for collateral, while lenders can earn interest on their lending capacity without the risk of default. Credit delegation also promotes financial inclusion and allows users to lend to trusted parties who may not have access to traditional financial services.

Tokenomics

AAVE is a decentralized finance (DeFi) platform that operates on the Ethereum blockchain. AAVE's native token is the AAVE token, an ERC-20 token used for governance and utility token on the platform. AAVE holders have the ability to participate in governance by voting on proposals to change various parameters of the AAVE protocol, such as collateral requirements, interest rates, and other governance aspects.

One unique feature of AAVE's tokenomics is the concept of "protocol fees". When borrowers take out loans on the AAVE platform, they pay an interest rate on their borrowed assets. A portion of this interest rate is taken as a fee by the protocol and sent to a separate smart contract known as the "Safety Module". These fees are used to purchase AAVE tokens from the open market and are then locked up in the Safety Module for a specified period.

The Safety Module is designed to act as an insurance fund, providing a buffer against losses in the event of a black swan event, such as a smart contract vulnerability or a sudden market downturn. In the event of a shortfall in the AAVE protocol, AAVE tokens held in the Safety Module can be sold on the open market to cover the shortfall and ensure that lenders are made whole.

Another important feature of AAVE's tokenomics is the "Staking Incentives" program. In this program, users who stake their AAVE tokens in the AAVE protocol are eligible to receive a portion of the protocol fees collected by the platform. The more AAVE tokens a user stakes, the greater their share of the protocol fees. This incentivizes long-term investment in the AAVE protocol, as well as aligning the interests of AAVE holders with the success of the platform.

Finally, AAVE has implemented a "Burn Mechanism" for the AAVE token. Whenever a user pays off a loan on the AAVE platform, they have the option to pay the interest portion of the loan in AAVE tokens instead of the borrowed asset. These AAVE tokens are then burned, reducing the total supply of AAVE in circulation. This mechanism ensures a deflationary pressure on the AAVE token and helps to maintain its value over time.

AAVE's tokenomics has two main utilities, governance and staking. The protocol is operated and governed by the token holders in the form of a DAO, with governance power proportional to the token balance. The governance function is used to submit and support improvement proposals that cover topics such as changes in risk parameters for the AAVE markets, the amount of tokens issued by the ecosystem reserve fund for safety or ecosystem incentives, and how to allocate treasury funds.

The second utility is staking, which involves users staking their tokens into the Safety Module (SM) to provide funds that can be used to secure the protocol. In exchange users get a reward paid in AAVE tokens that is issued by the ecosystem reserve. The percentage of the bonus is periodically decided by governance, and these token emissions are classified as safety incentives or SI. The safety module plays a crucial role in protecting the protocol against shortfall events that can occur due to unexpected losses of funds stemming from smart contract risks, oracle failure, and liquidation risk. In this case, the SM can use up to 30% of its funds to stabilize the protocol.

AAVE's tokenomics has been designed with the aim of incentivizing long-term participation in the protocol and ensuring its stability. The protocol has been battle-tested and has proven to perform well during extreme market conditions. Overall, the tokenomics of AAVE provides a powerful incentive mechanism for users to participate in the governance and security of the protocol, while also creating value for its token holders

Figure 33: AAVE tokenomics illustration (simplified)

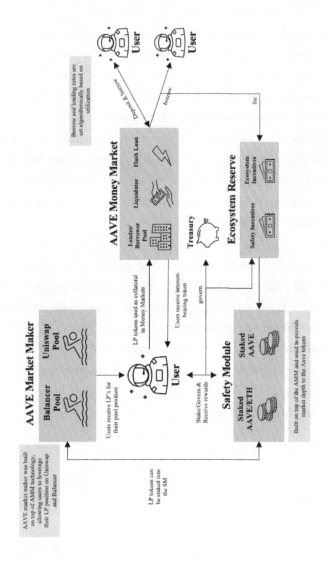

1. Liquidity

Liquidity is one of the most important factors for the success of any lending and borrowing platform. In the case of AAVE, attracting and retaining liquidity is essential to provide its users with a seamless experience. AAVE has employed various strategies to attract and retain liquidity.

One of the primary methods of attracting liquidity is through the issuance of its native AAVE token. These tokens are distributed to incentivize usage of the protocol and encourage liquidity providers to participate in the AAVE ecosystem. The ecosystem reserve fund, which received 3 million tokens from the genesis supply, invests in the AAVE ecosystem and issues tokens for rewards and incentives.

In addition to token incentives, AAVE has implemented liquidity pools on top of Automated Market Maker (AMM) technologies. This allows Uniswap and Balancer liquidity providers to use their LP tokens as collateral on the AAVE protocol. By doing so, AAVE can tap into a larger pool of potential customers and attract more liquidity.

AAVE also has a unique feature called the Credit Delegation. This feature allows users to delegate their credit lines to others, meaning that borrowers can take out loans using the credit lines of other users who have delegated their credit. This increases the liquidity available on the platform and provides more opportunities for users to earn interest on their funds.

Another factor that contributes to AAVE's liquidity is the protocol's ability to accept a wide range of assets as collateral. AAVE currently supports over 20 assets, including stablecoins and cryptocurrencies. This broad range of accepted assets ensures that there is a diverse pool of collateral available on the platform.

2. Token Distribution

AAVE has taken a unique approach to its token distribution, fully embracing decentralization from the outset. While many crypto projects reserve a significant percentage of their total supply for the founding team, advisors, and investors, AAVE has distributed all of its tokens to the community. However, it is essential to note that AAVE did not start out fully decentralized. The protocol underwent a gradual decentralization process, with governance keys being officially handed over to the community in 2020.

The current token distribution reflects AAVE's commitment to decentralization. The safety module, which represents staked tokens, is the largest holder, followed by the ecosystem reserve fund. The largest individual address holding AAVE holds just over 250,000 tokens, which represents only 1.6% of the available supply. This low percentage ensures that no single holder or group of holders can easily reach a majority to enforce their will, providing a truly democratic vote.

This decentralization level is a notable contrast to its biggest competitor, Compound, where the founding team and investors still own nearly 50% of the tokens. AAVE's fully decentralized token distribution ensures that the protocol's governance and operations are truly community-driven. It allows for equal participation in decision-making and ensures that no single entity holds too much power or influence over the protocol's future direction.

3. Value creation

AAVE creates value through various mechanisms, including the fees collected from lending and borrowing activities, token appreciation, and ecosystem growth.

First, the fees collected from lending and borrowing activities generate revenue for the protocol. AAVE charges borrowers an interest rate and requires them to put up collateral, ensuring that the protocol remains overcollateralized and secure. Lenders receive interest on their deposited funds, and the protocol takes a percentage of the interest as a fee. These fees are distributed to AAVE token holders through a buyback and burn mechanism, where tokens are purchased from the open market and burned, reducing the total supply and potentially increasing the value of each remaining token.

Second, AAVE token appreciation can also create value for its holders. As the demand for AAVE's services and its tokens grows, the price of AAVE may appreciate, allowing holders to benefit from the price increase.

Third, ecosystem growth is essential for AAVE's long-term value creation. The protocol has implemented various incentive programs to encourage participation and development within the ecosystem. The ecosystem reserve fund invests in projects and initiatives that promote AAVE's growth and development. The AAVE Grants program provides funding for projects that build on top of the protocol or contributing to its development. Additionally, the AAVE Improvement Proposal (AIP) process allows token holders to suggest and vote on changes to the protocol, enabling continuous improvement and innovation.

Besides constantly innovating in its lending and borrowing functionalities, AAVE sets itself apart from the other popular Ethereum lending protocols by heavily incentivizing the development of a multichain strategy and a diversified ecosystem. AAVE started on Ethereum, which is still its main market but has managed to expand to many other chains. This multichain strategy has enabled AAVE to reach different communities across the space and offer the broadest token selection for lenders.

In its V3 version, the protocol provides new features, like an interoperability function called Portal, which allows the flow of liquidity between AAVE V3 markets across different networks. More specifically, it will enable governance-approved bridges to burn aTokens on the source network while instantly minting them on the destination network.

In terms of value capture, as with most platforms, AAVE has a treasury where a portion of the spread earned from lending and borrowing plus the fees it charges from flash loans are deposited (Figure 33). These funds are governed by AAVE token holders. It's worth mentioning that the value captured by fees is reflected in the token by governance rights.

4. Demand Drivers

AAVE's native token, AAVE, offers two main utilities within its ecosystem: governance and staking. However, beyond the ecosystem, there are also several use cases for AAVE. For instance, it can be deposited on Maker to create DAI, used to provide liquidity on Balancer and earn BAL rewards or on Uniswap to earn trading fees. Furthermore, the governance forum of AAVE is continuously discussing the addition of more utilities to the token. Mark Zeller, an influential team member, has stated that as AAVE embraces the multiverse, new possibilities for utilities can be unlocked, positively impacting the demand for the token.

The governance power of the token and its reasonable staking reward give AAVE the potential to create an evolving ecosystem with many possibilities for further development. For instance, as the demand for L1 assets increases, there is the possibility of an "AAVE chain" linked to all networks with portals, allowing for cheap and fast usage of AAVE. In this scenario, validators must stake AAVE to process transactions and earn fees from network transactions. Additionally, bridges and protocols using the portals may be required to own amounts of StkAAVE to reduce fees and/or credit lines.

While the current stage of the token's utility may not be a decisive demand factor due to its low staking rate relative to the circulating supply and only paying out the native token, the protocol's fees generated go into the treasury, which token holders have control over. Although the protocol does not redistribute much of the value it creates to its users like Balancer, Curve, and GMX, it manages its treasury with a long-term view, placing AAVE in its leadership position.

Conclusion

It is clear that AAVE is a highly competitive leader in the decentralized finance (DeFi) sector. The platform's constantly evolving ecosystem, well-designed economic incentive program, and secure smart contract structure make it an attractive option for investors and users alike. Additionally, AAVE's token distribution is highly decentralized, with the majority of tokens held by the community and long-term holders who stake their tokens to secure the protocol, resulting in a healthy economic co-dependency between the protocol and its stakeholders. This alignment is crucial for making decentralized decisions on critical aspects of the platform, such as risk parameters, economic investments, and asset listings.

Moreover, AAVE's ecosystem incentives are geared towards liquidity providers and developers, who are the key stakeholders of the protocol, as they provide the liquidity, security, and development expertise to expand and integrate AAVE into the broader crypto ecosystem. These incentives create more value for AAVE's users and encourage greater participation in the platform.

Overall, AAVE's impressive array of features and mechanisms make it a strong contender in the rapidly growing DeFi space. As the ecosystem continues to evolve and expand, AAVE's innovative approach to value creation through its decentralized governance and economic incentives positions it well for continued success.

There are several potential risks that AAVE might face in the future. One significant risk is related to regulatory challenges, as the cryptocurrency industry is still relatively new and faces constant scrutiny from regulatory bodies. Any significant regulatory changes or restrictions could potentially harm the AAVE ecosystem and decrease demand for its services.

Another risk is related to the competition in the DeFi space, as there are several other lending protocols that offer similar services. As the DeFi ecosystem grows and evolves, AAVE will need to continue to innovate and differentiate itself to maintain its market share.

Additionally, there is always the risk of smart contract vulnerabilities or security breaches, which could potentially result in the loss of user funds or damage to the reputation of the AAVE ecosystem.

On the other hand, there are several growth opportunities for AAVE. One potential area for growth is in expanding the range of assets that can be borrowed and lent on the platform. AAVE has already taken steps in this direction by adding support for several new assets, but there is still room for expansion.

Another opportunity is to continue to develop and integrate with other DeFi protocols and services, creating a more interconnected ecosystem that offers more utility for users. This could potentially increase demand for AAVE and make it a more integral part of the DeFi landscape.

Finally, AAVE could explore partnerships and collaborations with traditional financial institutions, such as banks and investment firms, to bridge the gap between traditional finance and DeFi. This could potentially expand the user base and bring more liquidity into the AAVE ecosystem.

Optimism

O ptimism is a Layer 2 scaling solution that aims to bring low fees, fast transactions, and scalability to Ethereum. It operates as a rollup, which means that it aggregates multiple transactions into a single one and submits it to the Ethereum mainnet for settlement. This allows for a significant increase in the number of transactions processed per second while also reducing gas costs.

The Optimism team began its development in 2019 under the name Plasma Group. The initial goal of the project was to create a Layer 2 solution that could scale Ethereum to support a billion users. The Plasma Group was backed by prominent investors such as Coinbase Ventures, Paradigm, and Polychain Capital.

In 2020, the project rebranded as Optimism and started working on its main product, the Optimistic Rollup. The

Optimistic Rollup is a Layer 2 scaling solution that is built on Ethereum and uses a unique technology called Fraud Proofs to ensure the security and integrity of transactions.

The Optimistic Rollup operates by aggregating multiple transactions into a single one and then publishing it to the Ethereum mainnet. This single transaction is then verified by the Optimism network, which checks it against a set of rules that ensure the transaction is valid. Once the transaction is validated, it is added to the Optimistic Rollup, which acts as a temporary storage for transactions.

The Optimistic Rollup can process up to 2,000 transactions per second, which is a significant increase compared to Ethereum's current capacity of around 15 transactions per second. Furthermore, the gas fees on the Optimistic Rollup are much lower than those on Ethereum, making it an attractive option for users who want to save on transaction fees.

The technology behind the Optimistic Rollup is based on Fraud Proofs, which are mathematical proofs that ensure that all transactions in the Optimistic Rollup are valid. Fraud Proofs allow the Optimism network to be highly scalable while maintaining a high level of security.

Fraud Proofs present evidence that a state transition was incorrect. They reflect an optimistic view of the world: the assumption is that blocks represent only correct states of L2 data, until proven otherwise. In reality, a committed block could well include an incorrect state transition.

The main advantage of Fraud Proofs is that they are not needed for every state transition, but only when things supposedly break down. As such, they require fewer computational resources, and are a better fit for a scalability-constrained environment. The main disadvantage of these protocols stems from their interactivity: they define a 'conversation' between multiple parties. A conversation requires the parties — the party claiming fraud, in particular — to be present (liveness), and allows other parties to interrupt the conversation by various means. But the heart of the problem is the protocol's interpretation of silence (the absence of a challenge to a new state) as implicit consent. Indeed, an attacker could attempt to create the semblance of silence with DDoS attacks.

Since its launch, the Optimistic Rollup has achieved several milestones. In March 2021, the network launched its first testnet, which allowed developers to test their applications on the Optimistic Rollup before its mainnet launch. In July 2021, the Optimistic Rollup launched its mainnet, which marked a significant milestone in the development of the project.

Currently, the Optimistic Rollup is being used by several DeFi protocols, including Uniswap, Synthetix, and Chainlink. As the demand for Layer 2 scaling solutions continues to grow, the Optimistic Rollup is well-positioned to become a major player in the Ethereum ecosystem.

Tokenomics

Optimism's token, OPT, plays a vital role in the governance and operation of the Optimism network. The OPT token is an ERC-20 token that runs on the Ethereum network, and it is used to incentivize and reward validators who secure the network and participate in the governance process.

The total supply of OPT is capped at 100 million tokens, with no new tokens to be created. The initial token distribution was conducted through a seed round and a private sale to strategic investors, with the public sale scheduled for later in 2022.

Validators on the Optimism network must stake OPT tokens to participate in the network's consensus mechanism, which is based on a variant of the Proof of Stake (PoS) algorithm. Validators who participate in consensus and validate transactions are rewarded with OPT tokens, which incentivizes them to act in the network's best interests and maintain its security and reliability.

In addition to participating in consensus, OPT token holders also have a say in network governance. OPT holders can use their tokens to vote on network proposals, which cover topics such as network upgrades, fee structures, and other critical decisions that affect the network's operation and development.

One unique aspect of Optimism's tokenomics is its use of a decaying rewards system. The rewards for validators and other network participants gradually decrease over time, which incentivizes early participation and rewards long-term commitment to the network.

Decaying rewards work by gradually decreasing the rewards earned by stakers over time, with the goal of encouraging long-term participation and discouraging short-term speculation. The decaying rewards system is designed to reward early adopters and long-term stakeholders while also incentivizing ongoing participation in the network. At the same time, it discourages short-term speculation and encourages users to take a long-term view of their stake in the network.

The rewards earned by stakers are calculated based on the amount of tokens staked and the length of time they are staked. The longer a user stakes their tokens, the more rewards they will earn. However, as time goes on, the rewards earned by stakers will gradually decrease.

> *This system is designed to promote a stable and sustainable ecosystem by encouraging users to take a long-term view of their stake in the network. It also helps to prevent sudden fluctuations in the value of the network's token by discouraging short-term speculation and encouraging a more stable and steady increase in the token's value.*

Furthermore, a portion of the fees generated by the Optimism network is used to buy back OPT tokens, which helps to support the token's value and incentivize long-term holding. This buyback mechanism reduces the circulating supply of OPT, which, in turn, increases its scarcity and can lead to price appreciation over time.

Token Distribution

Optimism has taken a unique approach to its token distribution by implementing airdrops to both new and existing users. This distribution mechanism is designed to incentivize early adoption and to reward those who have already been using the platform.

One aspect of Optimism's airdrop strategy is the retrospective airdrop, which rewards users who have already interacted with the platform in the past. The retroactive airdrop program is designed to reward users who were early adopters of the platform and have helped to grow the ecosystem.

Optimism's token distribution strategy also includes a series of ongoing airdrops to new users, which are aimed at encouraging adoption and growth of the platform. These airdrops are designed to reward users who interact with the protocol and stake their tokens to provide liquidity to the ecosystem.

The tokens distributed through Optimism's airdrop programs are used to incentivize users to participate in various activities on the platform, such as staking and governance. Token holders have the ability to participate in platform governance by voting on proposals and decisions related to the platform's future development.

Utility

Optimism's native token, OPT, has a number of utilities within the protocol's ecosystem. The main utility is governance, which gives token holders a say in the direction and future development of the Optimism platform. OPT holders can submit and vote on proposals for upgrades, changes to protocol parameters, and other important decisions related to the platform. The governance system is set up so that OPT holders who stake their tokens have more voting power than those who don't, which incentivizes long-term holding and engagement with the protocol.

Another utility of OPT is for payment of transaction fees on the Optimism network. This is similar to how gas fees are paid on the Ethereum network, except that OPT is used as the native currency instead of ETH. This means that users can use OPT to pay for transactions on any dApps or services that are built on the Optimism network. It's worth noting that the fees on the Optimism network are significantly lower than those on the Ethereum network, which makes it an attractive option for users looking to save on gas costs.

Additionally, OPT is used as collateral for the Optimism Gateway, which allows users to move assets between the Ethereum network and the Optimism network. When users deposit assets into the Gateway, they receive an equivalent amount of Wrapped OPT (WOPT) tokens, which are used as collateral. If the user wants to withdraw their assets from the Gateway, they must first repay the amount of OPT that they borrowed against their deposited assets. This creates a demand for OPT as users need to hold in order to use the Gateway.

Despite these use cases, there has been some skepticism about the long-term utility of OPT as a token. Some argue that governance and transaction fee payment are not enough to create a strong and sustainable demand for the token.

Additionally, similar to other governance tokens, the majority of OPT tokens are held by a small number of whales, which could lead to centralization and reduced participation in the governance process.

Third Part

Best Practices

GameFi Tokenomics

G ames have been around for a very, very long time. Since the dawn of human lifeform, there has been evidence of our seemingly intrinsic infatuation with games. Prehistoric and ancient civilizations initially used bones to mold the early forms of dice. The first pair of dice, found in the Shandong Province, have been dated back to 5,000 years ago and, quite interestingly, had fourteen irregular sides as opposed to the contemporary six. The evolution of dice serves as just one example of how gaming has played an important role throughout human history.

Perhaps, the most influential type of games throughout human history has been video games. The origin of video games began in the 1950s as computer scientists began designing simple games and simulations on minicomputers and mainframes. Soon after came the first home video game console - the Magnavox Odyssey - and the first arcade video games - Computer Space and Pong. It wasn't until the 1990s, however, that we saw the introduction of optical media via CD-ROMs and real-time 3D polygonal graphic rendering.

Games have always been one of the ways for us to adopt different technologies - Microsoft Solitaire was there in the '90s to teach us how to use a mouse to click, drag and drop, and interact with the graphical user interfaces, and now it has become almost intuitive. Sony's decision to include a Blu-ray player in their PlayStation 3 was one of the deciding factors for the high-definition optical disc format war between HD DVD and Blu-ray. It is likely that many people use a VR headset for the first time because of the immersive gaming experience. Games will likely do the same for blockchain technologies by educating users on how to operate a wallet, pay gas fees for transactions and interact with smart contracts.

From the 2000s and into the 2010s, casual gaming and streaming have become an overwhelming force in the gaming industry, embodying a much more mainstream consumer. The industry has shifted to mobile gaming on smartphones and tablets instead of handheld consoles. Additionally, gaming has touched almost every geographic region of the world and is growing outside the traditional bounds of North America and Western Europe.

In 2022, a staggering 3.2 billion players are expected to consume video games, leading to an estimated US$185 billion in generated revenue. By 2025, this number will grow even further, reaching around 3.5 billion players and generating around US$210 billion.

While the coronavirus pandemic remains a harsh reality in some parts of the world, many countries have lifted their restrictions. This means that consumers are no longer confined to their homes and readily participate in activities that were part of their lives before COVID-19. Naturally, we have seen a slight slowdown in the growth of games sold this year compared to 2020 and 2021. However, engagement with games is sticky, as many gamers tend to form bonds with characters, storylines, and gaming objectives. We anticipate gaming to continue to grow in the long run, despite recent falls in engagement in the short run.

The essence of gaming is ingrained in the human fabric. As shown by the evolution of dice and video games, gaming constantly evolves and adapts to whatever technological medium is most pervasive at the time. For these reasons, it is advisable to pay close attention to how gaming takes form in a blockchain environment.

Figure 34: Global Gaming Market Share

Source: Newzoo.com

If we consider tablet and smartphone games as one broad mobile market, we can see that this category accounts for more than 50% of the total US$200B+ market this year. Looking closely at the geographical split, Asia Pacific is by far the biggest market. That being said, Latin America, the Middle East & Africa are both growing fast and will likely account for a larger share in the coming years.

Figure 35: Global Gaming Distribution

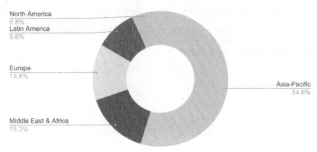

Source: Newzoo.com

One area of gaming that has already proven to be well-suited to a blockchain environment is play-to-earn (P2E) games. P2E refers to games that effectively pay you for playing the game. P2E is not a completely new concept to gaming - gold farming in World of Warcraft was widely reported more than 10 years ago. The ownership of assets and freedom of transfer from blockchain technologies make it more feasible. More specifically, P2E games on the blockchain offer cryptocurrency in return for in-game achievements, items, and other forms of engagement. To pay players, most P2E games require users to provide a crypto wallet at the point of registration.

In its current form, the P2E space feels relatively immature; The market is dominated by financially-oriented P2E titles whose core focus is on experimenting with economic incentives rather than the gameplay itself. Consequently, most of the current games are plagued with sustainability issues. Players are not incentivized to engage with the games for reasons other than financial gain, leading to a system that can only sustain itself if there is a continuous influx of players (and funds) into the game. As a result, P2E gaming has received much criticism from the gaming community.

However, it is important to remember that this kind of progression is natural. Gaming requires time to evolve and become more complex (just as we moved from dice to pong to full-story RPGs). As time passes, we will see more competition in the P2E space. As a result, blockchain gaming will attract top developers and ultimately challenge traditional AAA titles in terms of technical complexity and player base. More importantly, we will witness how blockchain technology's benefits enhance gaming in its current form to become more engulfing and compelling. We must explore what qualities make a good game to overcome the current shallowness in the P2E blockchain games space.

If you are a game developer, you will know that designing a successful game is an incredibly difficult feat. A successful game must be engaging and stimulating in ways other games aren't. A successful game must be continuously alluring, leading players to come back time and time again to accomplish in-game tasks. At the same time, a game can have the best graphics, gameplay, and control, e.g., Star Wars™ Battlefront™ II, but it can be ruined by an in-game economy that encourages pay-to-win.

For games built on the blockchain, there is another idiosyncratic requirement to creating a successful game: Complementary tokenomics. Incorporating tokenomics into a game adds a new layer of complexity for game developers. The tokenomics must complement the overall game design - If tokenomics are carelessly integrated, player incentives become easily misaligned and may overshadow a game's inherent value.

There are a few best practices in designing a game that we should have a closer look at.

1. Challenges

Who doesn't love a good challenge? Demon's Souls, for example, is known as one of the hardest games, contributing to its overall appeal to players. A good game designer gives his players continuous challenges to keep them hooked on playing a game. The goal is that most of these challenges satisfy some learning objectives. This could include answering questions, completing a portion of a map, or obtaining a new in-game item. As a general rule, good games should be easy to learn, but hard to master.

2. Flexibility

Everyone has their own way of going about things, and limiting a gamer's way of solving puzzles can often lead to more frustration than people expect. Thus, allowing for flexibility, by ensuring that there are many different ways to accomplish each goal, is important. Instead of designing a step-by-step progression, it is best to let each player work out their own strategy to the endpoint while still keeping the game challenging.

3. Rewards

Successful players can be granted new capabilities, skills, and equipment to make the game feel rewarding. In-game rewards can be surprisingly motivating to players. The value of the game is not just to win it, but also to keep playing and to collect rewards. One challenge that most game designers face is finding the perfect balance of difficulty and reward.

4. Entertainment

Excessive realism can be boring. There is nothing wrong with making some incorrect assumptions about how the world works or allowing for unrealistic behaviors or skills. Most gamers are looking for an escape from reality, and fun is a crucial element that makes them return to the games they're playing. It is the element of fun and challenge that makes gamers return. We should keep this in mind when thinking about how to design a sustainable GameFi experience.

5. Controls

Even if everything about your game is amazing, it won't matter if your players can't properly interact with it. Therefore, designing controls that fit the game and enhance the experience is one of the key elements of fostering an addictive game experience. This also includes any usage of tokens within the game. They should be intuitive to use and not introduce new barriers to entry. If any of you remember Super Mario 64, you will know what we mean when we talk about great controls. If the main game mechanics aren't fun, your game may as well have been a movie.

6. Captivating Worlds

Nailing down the gameplay is certainly important. However, the visuals of a game and creating captivating worlds still remain a critical secondary component to a game's success. Skyrim and The Legend of Zelda are examples of games that have created not only stunning visuals but also a world that is captivating and fascinating. The best games usually have a level design that serves to complement the main game mechanics. Well-planned levels will help push the story forward while keeping players engaged as they face new challenges.

In addition, whether your game is heavy on narrative or not, your game should contain interesting and memorable characters. You want to be able to relate to the protagonist. This means designing characters that are visually interesting, well-written, and that the player can relate to. Most storytellers would even argue that the characters, not the plot or setting, separate a good story from a great one. After all, humans love being touched, entertained, and encouraged by intriguing stories with memorable characters, plot twists, and more. Since games are interactive, they are also capable of serving as an incomparable storytelling medium.

7. Something Different

Last but not least, it's great if games are unique. While following the same formula of another great game may seem like a profitable idea, it's the games that introduce something unique that captivates audiences. Every game designer should strive to create a game that offers a new experience that players can't get anywhere else, even if it means just adding a few tweaks to an already-existing genre or style of game.

It is evident that there are a lot of elements that are needed when designing an amazing game. This makes it all so clear why the job of a game designer is anything but easy. Further, adding crypto to this equation adds another layer of complexity, making it even harder to achieve all of the aforementioned aspects while also maintaining sustainable and effective tokenomics.

Figure 36: The Seven Pillars of Game Design

Gaming in a Crypto Context

At this point, we understand a bit better what it takes to design a good game. However, putting a good game into the context of crypto adds new layers of complexity. Looking at gaming in a more crypto-native context, we can see that the primary reason people want to engage is still similar to traditional gaming. It is not for financial benefits but for playing a fun and entertaining game. After all, users are willing to invest time to install, set up the game, and learn how to operate it. As such, we can crystalize fun and entertainment as key elements for crypto native games as well. While this is a requirement for almost all games to be successful, the introduction of tokenomics and blockchain technology can often distract from this fact.

Let's look at it more in-depth in a crypto-native context. Non-fungible tokens (NFTs), if available in the game, can be seen as tools with in-game utilities. They could be collectibles (artwork worth collecting with potential use-case across platforms, like StepN Asics sneakers instead of the random-looking sneakers) or items that offer some form of utility. Interestingly, a majority of blockchain primitives (such as ERC-721) have been motivated by traditional gaming. Vitalik Buterin, explained that one of the main motivations for him to create a non-fungible token standard was a World of Warcraft (WoW) update. In 2010 the WoW patch 3.1.0 made him "realize what horrors centralized services can bring", motivating him to create Ethereum just two years later and allow for items also to have non-fungible characteristics.

Retention rate is one of crypto game developers' most important key performance indicators (KPIs). This is very similar to the free-to-play realm, where we often have monetizing in the form of advertisements. When exactly you measure your retention rate is up to you — and varying this can lead to valuable information on your game's performance. Measuring a one-day retention rate shows if you are effectively onboarding new users and will let you know what kind of first impression your game makes on people who have just downloaded it. In contrast, a seven-day retention rate helps you to determine how much people like your app — looking at drop-off from day one to day seven is a valuable insight into app performance and will help determine how long people will play your game or use your app. After a month, expect your user base to have shrunk dramatically. Users remaining will likely be using the game regularly and are a valuable revenue driver — this is the ideal segment to target with crypto-native games.

A current barrier to use for crypto games is the need for a web3 wallet connection. Considering that time being spent on installing and setting up a game can impact sales (mobile games have a huge advantage here), it is important to note that within the GameFi space, ease of use should be at the center of attention.

Assuming that the GameFi space will evolve more going forward, I expect more high-quality games to be introduced into the market. Games of similar quality should attract gamers from traditional markets and thus set up the crypto gaming space as a key entry point for people into web3 and crypto.

To understand the need for strong and sustainable tokenomics better, let us look at the value that blockchain technology brings to the gaming industry.

1. Digital Asset Ownership

There are significant benefits to users who choose to dabble into GameFi: Ownership over your assets, the ability to earn rewards while playing, and decentralized governance power are just a few.

Let's take the popular video game Fortnite as an example. Fortnite is a free-to-play game that generates revenue from in-game purchases. Purchases made don't bring any extra benefits to the gameplay but are rather enhancements to the look of your characters, such as skins and accessories - the community element is crucial to the success of Fortnite. However, these skins are not unique, and there is no way to verify ownership. If Epic Games (the Fortnite game developer) wanted to permanently deactivate any skins purchased, they could easily do this and leave you stranded the same way World of Warcraft did with Vitalik. If you're deciding to quit the game and you're looking to sell your in-game purchases, you're often faced with a lot of challenges.

In comparison, let's take a closer look at a classic game built on the blockchain. Often, similar to Fortnite, players can either play the game for free with the ability to purchase skins. One key difference could be that unless you purchase a skin, you won't be able to earn rewards from playing the game. Additionally, unlike Fortnite skins, these skins are NFTs that are actually owned by the player. As the player increases in levels, the earning potential for the player increases as well, further increasing the value of the NFT simultaneously. If you wish to sell your skins, you can often do so through popular NFT marketplaces.

Having ownership over your assets could potentially mean that you can transfer your skins, avatars, or items into another game or across games developed by the same project and give you more freedom than you had before.

2. Governance

Another key aspect to look at is that of control. Heading back to the Fortnite example, the developers are the ones purely in control of the game's direction and roadmap. With emerging decentralized organizational structures like DAOs, crypto-native games can allow user-based input into the direction and roadmap of the game driven by tokenized ownership. The DAOs can not only help in steering development but also in the project's growth strategy with regards to capital and community. Tokens allocated to the DAOs treasury can be used for further development.

3. Decentralized Gaming Economies

By creating decentralized gaming economics, players gain the ability to receive a portion of the game revenue, which can lead to better player retention and lower customer acquisition costs. In addition to that, due to the decentralized nature, players don't have to rely on a centralized party and could potentially contribute to the game themselves.

4. Transparency

A key element of fraud prevention is avoiding what is known as the double spending problem. The double spending problem is the outcome of spending the same money more than once. Of course, there is a possibility that a digital currency can be spent twice, too, which would immediately turn them into useless code. As such, overcoming the double spending problem was a key milestone achieved with blockchain technology. Using cryptocurrencies, you don't need to depend on a third party to confirm your transactions. Instead, blockchain makes it possible to algorithmically solve the double-spending problem and also introduces the concept of digital scarcity.

Putting this into the context of crypto gaming, we can see that users had little insight into how the supply of their in-game currency was being managed. Consequently, they had limited understanding of how the value of their in-game currency was fluctuating. By double-spending or minting more in-game currency, hackers or even the game's developers themselves could increase the in-game currency supply without users knowing. As a result, users could be negatively impacted and blindsided by the dilution of their in-game currency holdings. In web3 games, there is much greater transparency into the supply side of in-game currencies. Web3 games are often accompanied by a whitepaper that almost always gives an in-depth breakdown of the in-game currencies' tokenomics. Additionally, the circulating supply and total supply can be verified by tracking the in-game currencies contract through block explorers. Lastly, blockchain technology in itself prevents double-spending by maintaining consensus amongst a group of validators/miners. As a result, no malicious actor can continuously spend the same in-game currency twice, or degrade the perception of the currency's value.

5. Royalties

Outside of user value, there is a lot of value derived for game developers, too. In the current model, game revenues are solely driven by the actual purchase of the game and then in-game purchases if available. Through embedded smart contracts, the blockchain-enabled model allows for revenue generation upon asset transfers as well, thus adding a new revenue stream for developers. Users are free to transfer assets as they please, with the developers generating revenue from transaction fees in the form of royalties (if they decide to do so). This and other monetization opportunities can be especially lucrative for developers. With blockchain games, creators generally retain much more of the value they create as well as benefit from on-chain royalties.

6. Economic Alignment

Giving players the ability to receive a portion of the game revenue should, in theory, lead to better player retention and lower customer acquisition costs. While still debatable, having a stake in the game can be seen as a net positive for players.

7. Unique Developer Controls

Developers can regulate their gaming economies effectively through smart contracts, setting specific predefined conditions to control trading within their games. This ensures that trades are conducted fairly and can limit the over-saturation of the in-game market.

Blockchain platforms could potentially also provide a safer and more secure environment to build on. They use powerful data encryption technologies to secure transactions, and hackers can't destroy a decentralized blockchain network since there isn't a single centralized server or set of servers to destroy. On top of this, blockchain allows developers to communicate more openly with players and hear their feedback.

8. Composability

Composability is a key benefit for both users and developers. Allowing completely different games to interact with one another can help unlock new gaming use cases that have never been possible before. It can further alleviate the overall use cases for skins and NFTs. The key benefits often are most notable when looking at a single game developer as they can assure the composability of skins and operation on the same blockchain for the games they develop.

Figure 37: Benefits and Drawbacks of blockchain for Gaming

Pros	Pros
For developers • Player ownership of in-game assets • Ability to earn while playing • Ability to trade with secondary market liquidity • Decentralized decision making • On-chain reputation	• Risk of high barriers to entry • A high focus on economics gain might take away from the overall experience • Player onboarding can be difficult (need for crypto wallets) • Gaming community is still small (relatively speaking) • Concerns around sustainability
For developers • Increase Monetization options • Economic Alignment with users • Creator Economics • Increased visibility and funding • Composability	While some obstacles still exist (notably around the gameplay experience), we should expect them to be migrated as more resources and expertise are devoted to this space

What GameFi is missing

For the last two years, GameFi and P2E have been terms that have grown in popularity alongside the early success of projects such as StepN and Axie Infinity. Since then, many games have experimented with GameFi. However, most GameFi incentives currently require high emissions and have led to questions surrounding the sustainability of these systems. Before learning how to create more sustainable gaming Tokenomics, we must learn what GameFi and P2E actually entail.

So what actually is GameFi? GameFi is an acronym, combining the terms gaming and decentralized finance (DeFi"), and concerns how gameplay is monetized in a decentralized system. P2E projects allow players to obtain in-game rewards (usually tokens) by completing tasks and progressing through various game levels. Unlike traditional gaming rewards, self-custodial ownership over in-game rewards means that players have the ability to easily list rewards on decentralized marketplaces. Thus, allowing for the value of rewards to be easily traded on the open market. The financialization of blockchain gaming has proven to be powerful at attracting players. With the possibility of monetizing in-game rewards, crypto enthusiasts are onboarding onto games to earn rewards. This recent financialization of the gaming industry can represent a drastic change to traditional gaming, where the only incentive to play the game was the element of fun alone.

We can differentiate mainly between the two approaches. One is that of casual gaming, which is similar to many mobile games and focused on those who only play once in a while (e.g. during their commute back home). Another is that of AAA-rated games that focuses on those that actively seek out games as a free-time activity.

The first approach is casual gaming. People in this category might only play once in a while and enter the market for social aspects or to simply "kill some time". Casual gamers represent a big audience, and games targeted toward them should have low barriers to entry and simple controls. As such, especially for blockchain-native games, it is important to make the usage of tokens in the game easy. Sometimes this means that not everything needs to be done on the blockchain directly and that free elements are simple software code and NFT technology will only be utilized for paying customers.

One example of casual games is Axie Infinity - one of the largest P2E games on the blockchain. Players in Axie Infinity are tasked with collecting, breeding, and training creatures called "Axies." Eventually, players can put their Axies to the test by engaging in player vs. environment or player vs. player battles. Axie Infinity can be categorized as a casual game due to its widespread popularity and relatively informal gameplay. Axie Infinity established a two-token GameFi model, in which one token serves to provide in-game utility (SLP), and the other serves as a claim to engage in DAO governance (AXS). Years later, the two-token GameFi model has proven to become an industry standard and can be found across a plethora of games on the blockchain.

The second model of blockchain games is AAA-rated games. This model is the most likely to onboard typical gamers that aren't accustomed to the web3 space. There is a lot of hype around upcoming AAA-rated games, which are expected to have industry-grade gameplay. However, onboarding traditional gamers onto the blockchain might come with some barriers. As such, focusing on strong game design and industry-grade gameplay that is better than that of traditional platforms but utilizes blockchain technology might be the best approach here. Similar to casual games, in-game purchases should be seen as enhancements to the user experience and not create barriers that would make the game unenjoyable. AAA-rated games, compared to casual games, might prove to be more sustainable over the long run as they typically have a loyal customer base (similar to League of Legends) that enjoy the game for what it is. This should be an overall net positive as it most likely means that people are willing to hold tokens and NFTs for longer.

Illuvium is a highly anticipated, AAA-quality role-playing game. In the world of Illuvium, players are tasked with journeying across seven different graphically rich, alien landscapes to capture beasts known as Illuvials. Players in Illuvium can additionally wager on battles between Illuvials and purchase land to house and level up their Illuvials. Illuvium was created to fill the lack of "AAA gaming titles with cinematic quality 3D special effects" on the blockchain. As an AAA-rated game, players of Illuvium should expect high-quality visuals and game mechanics. Unlike Axie, Illuvium will follow a one-token GameFi model, in which it has only one native token ($ILV) for governance purposes. For in-game utility, Illuvium players will have to use ETH or convert their $ILV into synthetic $ILV (in a 1:1 ratio).

Designing a game while utilizing crypto is not easy. Tokenomics can often distract the developers as they don't focus on the key elements of what makes a good game. Simplifying the seven pillars outlined earlier, we can see how game developers aim to optimize for a trilemma between challenge, gratification, and engagement.

Figure 38: Web3 Gaming Trilemma

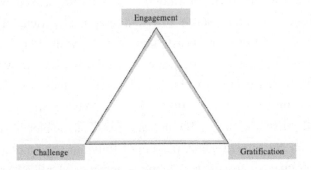

It is important for game developers to continue to emphasize all three of these aspects rather than just optimizing for one. Tokenomcis within a gaming ecosystem can introduce risks that limit the ability to optimize for these elements as control of the game's economy can be impacted. One key element to pay close attention to is sustainability.

One key issue that P2E games are facing is sustainability since a majority of players are putting too much focus on the ability to earn tokens rather than enjoying the game itself. As such, GameFi is currently in a stage where "mercenaries" are still part of the ecosystem, and while it will likely remain like this for the foreseeable future, it is important to onboard users that enjoy the game for what it is - a fun gaming experience.

Figure 39: Benefits and Drawbacks of Blockchain within Gaming

Pros	Cons
• Digital ownership • Secondary market liquidity • Improved funding • Community driven governance • Shared ownership structure	• Focus on mercenary behavior • Introduction of new complexity • Potential barriers to entry

Current web3 gaming projects are aiming to onboard gamers at a larger level, but so far, they are struggling to reach users in traditional markets. Mobile gaming offers one of the key markets that could be tapped into due to its ease of use. Especially if these games are integrated into an already existing web3 ecosystem. As our society becomes more digital and people across the world have increased access to affordable smartphones, successful GameFi projects on mobile could build huge user bases through simple tokenomics models.

As of now, however, a key focus has been on creating tokenomics without thinking about the sustainability of its mechanisms, which in a worst-case scenario, can create unsustainable token economics.

Figure 40: Unsustainable Token Economics

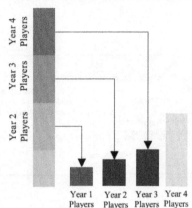

Token design becomes much more difficult when players develop avatars or characters over a long period of time, and their revenue depends on it. The reasons for this are manyfold. A few noteworthy reasons are:

- It is difficult to change the rules without user backlash (especially if this decision was driven by the developers and not the DAO)

- Wealth transfer from later players to earlier players is likely to occur in an unsustainable model

- Positive feedback is so strong that it is less tolerant of ecosystem contraction

How to create sustainable Tokenomics

Having looked at some key elements of the gaming ecosystem and blockchain space, let us dive into the main part of this report. How to create a sustainable GameFi project with good underlying tokenomics.

To facilitate token economics, a two- and n-token model can be used to separate the functionality of tokens. Two-token models are the most common form of a multi-token ecosystem. A two-token model provides two different tokens at the same time. This helps to specialize the use cases for each token by separating the "ecosystem" from a "purpose-solving" token. In most cases of two-token models, we have a utility token and a governance token. The utility token offers utility across most of the network to perform a specified task (e.g. to allow for in-game transactions). The governance token helps to decide on the directionality of a project by allowing to vote on proposals.

Governance Token - Governance tokens help to manage a protocol without impacting the price of the utility token. This becomes important when we consider use cases of a two-token model within games (amongst others) where the game design could be negatively impacted if a single-token model is used. If you want to make an in-game transaction (e.g. buy a collection item) but only have one token that is also used for governance, the game design might be negatively impacted due to speculation and price fluctuations. In extreme cases, this could lead to some gamers being excluded from the game due to high barriers to entry. As such, the main "task" of a governance token is to help separate the management of a decentralized project from the remaining aspects that should be considered.

Utility Token - This token is used only within the game. With this token, investors cannot raise funds as it is used to serve specific purposes based on the platform's architecture. Utility tokens could enable specific actions or provide specific rights within a platform or GameFi project. The best way to think about utility tokens is to imagine them as in-game currency, where you wouldn't want to see large price fluctuations to exclude a huge majority of gamers and have an infinite supply to be able to scale the game without negative impacts from scarcity.

Evaluating the benefits and drawbacks, I believe that less dilution of the governance token is a key advantage of a two-token model. Conceptually, when a reward is given in a second token, we shouldn't have a diluting effect on the first token. Furthermore, a separate utility token can allow for unlimited emission, which - especially for games - is a key aspect to consider. As such, a second token and a separation between governance and utility tokens can help to provide control over the inflation of the utility token. This, in return, is important since you want to be able to maintain a growing economy without leading to high barriers to entry due to high token prices. In addition, in some cases, supply restrictions would be favored by investors. As such, separating the use cases might help to tailor a token to the right audience.

Despite the benefits that a two-token model can bring, we also have to note some negatives. Use cases of a token are separated - which can lead to unnecessary complexity. Furthermore, this complexity can lead to wrong expectations. So far, some investors have expectations of tokens being somewhat correlated where it shouldn't be the case.

Depending on the use cases, each model offers some advantages and disadvantages. For some games, the advantages could outweigh the disadvantages when it comes to a two-token model. The separation between governance and utility tokens comes with important benefits for games - such as inflation control and incentive through fixed supply for investors. However, considering the above-mentioned downsides of two-token models, it should be enough for projects with well-designed tokenomics to function on a one-token model - especially if they leverage the usage of NFTs and other innovations. Especially if the game is truly fun to play. Ultimately, both offer two approaches that can work well depending on the specific design characteristics.

The Role of NFTs

Another aspect to look at is that of NFTs. NFT collectibles are perfectly suited for the GameFi space as they can represent characters, items, or even land. Owning an NFT to earn in P2E games is not always necessary, but in most cases, this is a way to maximize your income. Since every NFT is unique, this digital item is yours until you sell it.

A key question to ask around NFTs is whether or not people would be willing to hold them without the game built around them. While this should hold true for very popular games or unique designs, the majority of NFTs will likely be of little value outside of the game itself.

Another key element I also want to touch on is that of Sinks. Sinks and faucets aim to bring balance in value flow within a game. Simply put, sinks remove digital assets from circulation while faucets introduce them.

We can differentiate between two types of sinks

1. **Inflationary sinks** - What you pay is sunk immediately, but what you earn will be minted in the longer term
2. **Deflationary sinks** - A voluntary spend with no monetary benefits

Thinking about sinks and faucets from a web3 perspective we can see that introducing more and more inflationary sinks without a deflationary counterpart can be a dangerous endeavor since it might negatively impact the sustainability of a project.

That being said, together with deflationary sinks, the usage of sinks can bring a multitude of benefits since they incentivize traditional gamers to stay, given they leverage ownership and status. If players don't have an in-game activity to spend their tokens on, the supply of those tokens will create enough inflationary pressure to sink the price of the game's token. One of the simplest and most effective sinks is selling ultra-rare collectibles.

Targeted Token Model

> *Key idea: If a game cannot maintain a steady user retention ratio, it cannot be sustainable in the long run*

When designing GameFi tokenomics, a key aspect is their inflation design and overall sustainability. Similar to traditional games, the marketing budget is finite and has to rely on a constant stream of incentives to onboard renewable solutions for games on the platform. A key focus should be put on the overall innovation of the game design and gameplay aspects (new characters, skins, levels) that help to keep players engaged. As such, GameFi projects have a justification for a higher initial token allocation towards their treasury, as this helps to fund future development and growth.

There can be benefits to using two-token models as outlined above. Depending on the game design, splitting governance and utility tokens can benefit investors by decreasing the overall dilution and lead to a larger overall supply for user bootstrapping. However, I don't see two-token models as a requirement for crypto games. Instead, **for a game that is truly entertaining, a single token can be sufficient**. This can offer a multitude of benefits. Two noteworthy benefits are:

1. It minimizes the confusion and dilution of in-game utilities

2. It helps to focus market demand (and market-making resources) efficiently

Currently, the underlying issue with a two-token model is that it can lead to a downward spiral. As such, if developers incorporate tokens, they should be cautious that these tokens are designed in a way that avoids this. Furthermore, a two-token model relies on constant balancing between the two tokens, as can be seen with Axie Infinity which relies on a constant adjustment in the breeding fees in SLP and AXS to maintain the demand of both.

Another underlying drawback of a two-token model is managing the token prices of underlying tokens that have a large supply, which is a key risk factor that could cause a death spiral.

Figure 41: Death Spiral Scenario

To create a healthy balance I suggest the following: Restrict the reward token to a fixed percentage of the total supply to be distributed over a predetermined period (e.g. one year) to put a cap on the governance dilution.

To create a sustainable design, any future addition to the reward token allocation from the treasury or revenues should depend on key user and revenue metrics (e.g. calculate the cost of user acquisition, revenue per user, as well as % of paying users). Only once this is done the overall budget should be determined. A model of marginal diminishing returns should be considered.

Furthermore, an initial higher allocation towards the treasury and dev community can be justified to finance further development and innovation.

There is a justification for both one and two-token models, with both bringing their benefits and downsides. As such, the decision on the model should be made in a project-specific context. For a truly entertaining game, a single token can be sufficient. Just creating a two-token model without having designed a healthy mechanism can introduce new risks to a game.

User Bootstrapping

> **Key idea:** *Using the traditional game launch model to determine the go-to-market budget and initial % of the reward bucket*

Bootstrapping and onboarding new users are key elements for traditional and crypto-native games. The initial and ongoing user bootstrapping can often determine the overall success of a project and should thus play a key role in the overall strategy. An initial marketing budget should be comparable between traditional games and those that launch on a blockchain. The focus here is especially on the initial launch. Thus, I see the justification for an overall higher allocation towards a treasury or marketing allocation that is similar to that of traditional games.

AAA games - allocate 1:1 between marketing budget & development cost

Casual games - allocate ~25-50% of the development cost toward marketing

When thinking about user bootstrapping the initial goal should be to achieve a base layer of users that will create networks effect for the game. The below formula might help you to visualize your initial marketing budget:

$$\frac{Initial\ Launch}{Public\ Sale\ Market\ Capitalization} \times Reward\ Bucket\ \% = \frac{Initial\ Marketing}{Budget} = Early\ P2E\ Rewards$$

Reaching an initial 50,000-100,000 users is a key milestone for projects. Considering that retention rates can vary widely and customer acquisition costs can be higher for more complex (*and niche*) games a realistic assumption should be that 10-25% of users will be retained. Word-of-mouth marketing is a key aspect to consider to onboard further users in the future.

At its peak, StepN had around 3 million monthly active users (MAU) with a key part of the growth being driven by word of mouth.

Due to the niche nature and user behavior of GameFi, an overall higher acquisition cost for new users should be expected - slightly surpassing that of traditional mobile games. It is key that a healthy balance between the percentage dilution of ownership and the overall marketing is created. Once a healthy bootstrapping is created it is important that further incentives should come from the revenues generated and not from the treasury.

Revenue Accrual

> **Key idea:** *Revenue distribution and allocation should be structured in a way that rewards the long-term sustainability of the game*

Once the project is bootstrapped and a basic level of monthly active users is playing the game, it is important to manage revenue accruals in a way that is sustainable. As such, revenue distribution and allocation should be structured to reward long-term sustainability by incentivizing the team to continue developing the token, instead of using buyback and burn mechanisms that lead to a shrinking economy. While this benefits token holders in the short term, it contradicts the overall idea of sustainability in a GameFi context.

In most cases, revenue accrual should go exclusively (100%) to the DAO, which should be controlled by token holders.

Additionally, any revenue distribution at the token generation event should follow the below rules:

1. Allocate a percentage towards the "reward bucket" - This allocation should be used for tournaments, loyal rewards, and skilled players

2. Allocate a percentage to pay off development debt (if any)

3. Allocate a percentage towards a team bonus that will be available if specific milestones are achieved

Team Incentives

> ***Key idea:*** *Reward game development instead of token performance*

Let's continue talking about team incentives. The overall idea should be that team performance is encouraged not just by the overall token performance but by the game development instead. As such, in contrast to many games now, the key milestones should incentivize ongoing development, which allows for a more sustainable environment. Operational metrics such as the number of gamers, monthly active users, or key in-game developments (new levels, skins) should be at the forefront of this.

One way to do so is by agreeing to pre-defined milestones such as new maps, number of users, etc. It is important that these milestones will be adjusted by the DAO over time based on the overall performance and direction of the game. The goal should not be to make these milestones easier to reach but to create continuous motivation.

Game Lifecycle

> **Key idea:** *The DAO should act as the management and the supervisory board of the company looking at the long-term future of the project*

If we're looking at web2 Games, we can see that they often move in cycles and that the overall game lifecycle is limited if no innovation takes place. This is especially true if we compare console games (little to no change after release) to online and mobile games such as League of Legends, which expanded its lifecycle through constant innovation.

Figure 42: Google Trend Comparison for different Games

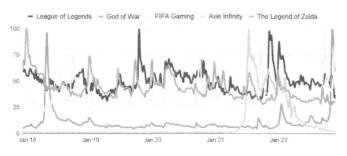

Source: Google

As we can see above, a game's lifecycle isn't infinite and only constant change and innovation (which is easier in mobile and online games) keeps the projects alive. That being said, looking at the traditional gaming space, revenue generated by sales from early games usually help to fund future projects.

Considering the lifecycle of games, a DAO should act as the management and board of directors of a company by focusing on the long-term future of the project. It is important to note that this future does not have to be defined by a single game, and can include many iterations of the same or different games. This can help to incentivize the community and core developers to stay invested in the project, thus prolonging the token life-cycle as well.

A few elements of games have also proven to prolong a game lifecycle and focusing on these elements can help to improve the overall sustainability of a project.

Social Elements - Creating communities and engaged members that come to the game not just for the graphic but for the community (similar to what Counter Strike and League of Legends have created) can help to add an additional element of "stickiness" to the game that can prolong the overall game lifecycle

Features - As mentioned above, bringing continued innovation to a game as well as introducing new features and content can help to increase the longevity of a project.

Once the popularity of a game has died, it can be proven helpful if the DAO and (the community behind it) allocate new bonus schemes out of the revenue towards content development. This is a key element to improve the need for the token. As such, we should think about tokens of gaming projects as a catalyst of continued innovation for games that people enjoy.

Inflation

> **Key idea:** *If rewards are funded by revenue in a controlled and calculated way inflation should not be a long-term issue*

While inflation might not always be an issue, it definitely is a key element to look at for two-token models. Inflation in the context of two-token models is important as inflation in the secondary token can trigger a downward spiral that could be hard to reverse once taken place.

In terms of inflation control, it is important to note that if the budget for initial rewards is fixed and any subsequent rewards are funded by the revenue generated (in a controlled way) then inflation should not be a long-term issue for the project.

However, selling pressure from an initial allocation towards a reward budget would still need to be mitigated. This could be done either by introducing vesting periods for the rewards (to give enough time for the players to get into the game and become loyal users) or by mercenary players absorbing the selling pressure. With enough control, the selling pressure should be reduced compared to the incentive rewards programming of the two-token model.

As we can see in Figure 42, reinvesting in the game and building continued improvements is a key way to mitigate inflation risk. As such, it is worth remembering is that if developers incorporate tokens, they should at least be cautious that these tokens do not trigger a downward spiral.

Token Utility

> **Key idea:** *Create demand for the token carefully in order to balance user adoption (free-to-play) and pay-to-win*

As mentioned in earlier chapters, utility is a key aspect of every tokenomics design. Within the gaming space, it is important to create a reason for the players to buy the token and play the game. In terms of tokens, the most direct way is by accepting the token as a medium of payment (rather than using a stablecoin).

In order to create utility and adoption outside of the crypto space and attract traditional gamers, fiat on-ramps can be important applications to help users to pay with credit cards - despite the underlying mechanism being crypto-native. As such, fiat should only enable you to buy the token which can in return be used to operate in-game transactions.

Figure 43: Fiat On-Ramp

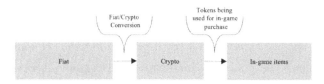

One element that needs to be considered here is that of know-your-customer (KYC), which is why it might be beneficial for the game to manage the fiat on-ramp steps for the players, rather than the players doing it themselves.

When thinking about designing a token economy, a developer is usually faced with the decision of whether to price everything in USD and have a token to pay for it or to price everything in the token directly.

If everything is priced in USD but paid with a native token, in the case of a price appreciation of the token, users may be reluctant to spend their tokens on in-game items. However, this could be balanced by introducing new rare items and constant innovation to the game that allows users to value the items higher.

For the second case, if everything is priced in the token and also paid for it with the token, we run the risk of creating an environment where the entry requirements will become higher as the token appreciates, creating an unfair gameplay experience and barriers to entry. The best solution is to price in USD since overall gameplay is less affected. This is in contrast to the majority of games now, however.

Currency distancing is a key aspect of in-game economic design. The goal is to de-couple the in-game currency from its underlying currency. One way to implement currency distancing is to limit the amount of currency players can earn from repetitive tasks, such as farming or grinding. This makes it less rewarding for players to spend all their time engaging in these activities and encourages them to explore other gameplay mechanics that may offer more diverse and engaging experiences.

Another strategy is to introduce alternate currencies that serve different purposes or are earned through different means. For example, players may be able to earn a currency specifically for completing story quests or engaging in PvP activities, which can be used to purchase unique rewards or unlock exclusive content. This encourages players to diversify their gameplay experiences and engage with other aspects of the game beyond just accumulating currency.

Some games also implement daily or weekly caps on the amount of currency that can be earned, which helps prevent players from grinding endlessly and encourages them to take breaks and explore other aspects of the game.

It is necessary to create a healthy balance between addictive, free-to-play elements and the pay-to-win characteristics of a game. Ideally, paying should only affect cosmetics (like League of Legends) and does not impact the gameplay itself. To go down this route, patience is a key element, as monetization will only happen over time as the popularity of the game progresses. For social games, paying should only increase the convenience, but not negatively impact the overall experience. To evaluate the effectiveness of parameters, a more quantitative way is appropriate. This could be based on traditional game data to predict user attraction, retention ratio, paying ratio, and revenue per paying user.

When a well-capitalized game studio wants to develop a web3 game without worrying about token design, there is also the option of not issuing new tokens at first and using only stablecoins like USDT and USDC, though this option would limit the overall design choices and mechanics of the game.

Figure 44: GameFi Token design Key Ideas Summary

Targeted Token Model	If a game cannot maintain a steady user retention ratio, it cannot be sustainable in the long run
User Bootstrapping	Using the traditional game launch model to determine the go-to-market budget and initial % of the reward bucket
Revenue Accrual	Revenue distribution and allocation should be structured in a way that rewards long-term sustainability of the game
Team Incentives	Reward game development instead of token performance
Game Lifecycle	The DAO should act as the management and the supervisory board of the company looking at the long-term future of the project
Inflation	If rewards are funded by revenue in a controlled and calculated way inflation should not be a long-term issue
Token Utility	Create demand for the token carefully in order to balance user adoption (free-to-play) and play-to-win

Conclusion

Designing games is hard. Designing games on the blockchain - while bringing a lot of new innovations - is harder. Incorporating tokenomics into a game adds a whole new layer of complexity for game developers. However, numerous benefits make it a worthwhile endeavor.

It is important for game developers to design tokenomics that truly complement the overall game design rather than being carelessly integrated. In a worst-case scenario, player incentives become misaligned and may overshadow a game's inherent value, which will negatively impact the overall longevity of the game.

While still in its early stage, web3 games will likely do for blockchain technologies what solitaire did for the computer in the 1990s - drive further adoption and education. By educating users on how to operate a wallet, pay gas fees for transactions and interact with smart contracts, crypto games are potentially the next key driver of growth and adoption within the crypto space.

Looking at the tokenomics element in more detail, fun and entertainment remain key elements to consider - tokenomics should add to this rather than distract from it. One key issue that P2E games are facing is sustainability since a majority of players are putting too much focus on the ability to earn tokens rather than enjoying the game itself. As such, while there a benefits to a two-token model, it isn't an underlying necessity for games to be successful. Truly fun games can design sustainable tokenomics with a single token alone.

One of the obvious challenges with creating sustainable web3 games is tokenizing all game assets without sacrificing control of the game's economy. It is important to keep in mind that just because an in-game asset can be turned into an NFT or fungible token, it doesn't mean it should be made into one. Instead, it is important to consider how this will impact the overall gaming experience and if there are net benefits to it. Each asset that is introduced within a game needs to justify its existence and bring value across user acquisition and retention.

Market Design

W hen thinking about design aspects, there are three important principles that we haven't touched on yet. These are thickness, congestion, and safety. All three help to create healthy market dynamics, and there are elements within tokenomics to consider contributing to each of these three.

1. Thickness

Thickness is the first element that we should touch on. A healthy market must have enough participants willing to transact and create benefits through trade and to further attract more participants. For example, buyers prefer to have access to many sellers, and vice versa. Generally, stores and shoppers are not interested in dead malls.

2. Congestion

A congested market is never good. As such, markets should mitigate jams to enable the free flow of transactions. Though this may be caused by an increase in thickness, it must be managed so that all participants have sufficient time to consider their options, or they may be forced to act on incomplete information.

3. Safety

Third, participants must feel safe to transact and to reveal their true preferences. Without proper safety, participants may wish to transact outside of the market or attempt to "game the system" which adds a barrier to entry for other participants.

Tokens can be used to help markets by increasing thickness, reducing congestion, and providing safety. Instead of thinking about if a system should require staking, it may be more meaningful to ask if a system's users require adequate market safety to comfortably transact.

Rather than blindly allocating mining rewards, a network can be tasked to achieve specific levels of network activity, or market thickness.

Increasing Thickness

1. Mining

Projects with tokens will often set aside a reserve of tokens for "mining," an activity which aims to reward behaviors that strengthen the network.

By disproportionately rewarding early adopters to spur network growth at the most critical junctures, a network can provide fair incentive to its participants scaled to the impact of their contributions towards growing a strong network economy. When the reserved portion of tokens are completely mined, the project is expected to have taken flight and able to sustain itself off of transaction fees alone. To put this another way, mining can be used to increase market thickness by shepherding network effects to sustainable steady states.

2. Partnerships

Strategic partnerships with organizations or companies in relevant industries can drive early adoption and bootstrap network effects. For example, in Uber's partnership with American Express, the ridesharing company provided credits to Amex cardholders to attract new users, while Amex could offer more benefits to its existing users. Likewise, some projects send pre-allocated or newly minted tokens to entice network participation. Networks that inflate their supply to build partnerships should only do so if the added value of the partnerships exceeds the cost of dilution across finances and control.

3. Referral Bonuses

More often than not marketplaces pay to have new users referred to them if the prospective increase in network value surpasses the payment amount. Reserved tokens can serve this purpose too, but at even steeper incentives as rewards may then scale to the benefits that the referrals bring to the network. One important concern that must be addressed is sybil attacks, in which attackers create many new fraudulent accounts to collect referral bonuses, thereby sapping the network of its resources without delivering value.

Reducing Congestion

1. Transaction Fees

Many token economies require the payment of network fees in tokens. When token prices are correlated to network value, it is more expensive to run the same transaction on a more valuable network. In general, popularity drives network value, and the resulting increase or decrease in token price can have a self-regulating effect on the congestion of transactions.

Those more willing to transact will offer higher fees to convince the network to give their transactions preferential treatment. In return, the higher fees may attract more transaction processors to eventually lower the fees. This works well when the value of a network activity to its participants is scaled to the fee they must pay, well-aligned with pricing theory - more use means more cost.

In the Ethereum blockchain, fees are paid in Gas per computation step taken in smart contracts, penalizing large programs while encouraging efficient programming. This fee structure is used to meter a rival good: the network has limited computational capacity, as all compute nodes on the network must run every smart contract, effectively limiting the network computational capacity to that of a single node. Scarce resources must be rationed, and fees can serve as mechanisms to do so.

Looking closely at congestion reveals an open problem in today's prominent decentralized networks to us: "*full nodes*" host and share the entire transaction histories of the network for free, yet they are critical to network performance and consistency. While there are incentives for the operation of full nodes, they are often not directly financial and difficult to model. For example, due to growing industry interest and the rapid pace of adoption, the Bitcoin network can take several hours to weeks for a full sync on commodity hardware. Furthermore, transactors pay once and forever replicate to all full nodes that join the Bitcoin network.

There are a few popular ways to mitigate congestion by leveraging market forces. The most popular include grading transactions, metering bandwidth, and charging access fees. Essentially, they create premium performance for those willing to pay, and create new revenue streams for node operators. They can also coexist with a free basic access layer to encourage widespread adoption.

2. Membership Deposits

When denominated in the native token, membership deposits can track the network value and provide scaling barriers to entry to discourage low-quality listings. With the assumption that membership quality is correlated with ability to put up entry fees, a network with rising value will have higher quality membership.

Providing Safety

1. Governance

Infrastructure, property ownership, and functioning legal systems are important components businesses need to thrive and create sustainable growth. If an enterprise were to leverage open-source technologies as its core building blocks, it would be at the whim of the project maintainers. Tokens can help businesses and individuals shape open-source development efforts through voting and similar mechanics. Because businesses have an interest in maintaining their underlying infrastructures, there is value in participatory rights as they can be used to secure a long-term development roadmap.

2. Smart Contracts

When tokens are augmented with smart contracts, they provide many computer-enforced guarantees around deal mechanics that must usually be drafted into legal contracts. For example, a good faith deposit implemented with a smart contract can be confirmed by all parties that the funds will be transferred to the payee upon deal expiry.

3. Attestations

Attestations are beliefs about reality that can be accounted. When they are used on a blockchain, they typically take the form of a digital reference to more concrete body of evidence. Examples of blockchain attestations:

- A signed digital reference to an image of a state-issued license for conducting Know Your Customer (KYC)

- A website address to an API on an official manufacturer's website which provides confirmatory responses to valid serial numbers, along with a cryptographic proof of the device's claimed serial number

- A phone number and business hours, regularly validated by reputable and independent 3rd parties

- A signed digital reference to a scanned PDF proof of $1MM in liability insurance

Attestations improve market safety by giving participants more knowledge about their prospective counterparties and therefore seeding trust. People feel safer dealing with people they can trust.

4. Staking

Staking requires network participants to put up safety deposits that may be arbitrated in a dispute. An arbiter may review a transaction and decide to award damages to a wronged party, paying from the safety deposit. Along with a safety deposit minimum, the network can effectively evict bad actors. When participants have "skin in the game," they are less likely to act erratically and put more thought before violating rules.

Tokenomics Evaluation Framework

I nvesting in crypto tokens can also be risky due to the volatility and lack of regulation in the market. Therefore, it is important for investors to conduct proper due diligence and evaluate the potential risks and rewards of investing in a particular token. It is worth it creating a personal tokenomics evaluation framework. This chapter is meant as a first introduction to help you create your own. In a later chapter, I will provide you with a short checklist that can also be used as a starting point for any further work you do in this regard.

Simply put, a good framework should consider several key factors that we touched on in this book, including token distribution, token utility, token economics, market dynamics, team and community, technical considerations, and regulatory considerations. A lot of this will already be familiar to you, but for completeness, let us summarize some of the key elements of a good token evaluation framework.

1. Token Distribution

Token Distribution refers to how the total supply of tokens is allocated. The distribution model can have a significant impact on market supply and demand, which ultimately affects the token's price. Investors need to know how many tokens are outstanding, how they are distributed, and who holds them. Token lock-up and vesting schedules are also important considerations.

2. Token Utility

Token Utility refers to the different use cases of the token within the project ecosystem. A well-designed token should have a clear and useful function that aligns with the project's goals. The utility of a token is an essential factor in driving demand and increasing the token's value. Token scarcity and how it impacts the token's value should also be considered.

3. Token Economics

Token Economics considers how tokens are created, distributed, and destroyed. The economics of a token can have a significant impact on its long-term value. Key metrics to evaluate in token economics include token inflation rate, deflationary mechanisms, and token velocity. Inflation and deflation mechanisms can significantly impact the token's long-term value. Token supply and demand also play a crucial role in token economics.

4. Market Dynamics

Market Dynamics refer to the market capitalization, trading volume, liquidity, and volatility of the token. These metrics give investors an idea of how much interest there is in the token, how much it's being traded, and how much it's worth. The broader market and competitive landscape also play a role in determining a token's potential value. Investors need to consider both short-term and long-term market dynamics to evaluate a token's potential value.

5. Team and Community

Team and Community behind a token are critical factors to consider. The team's experience, expertise, and credibility can significantly impact the token's success. Investors need to assess the team's track record, the strength of the project's partnerships, and the size and activity level of the community. A vibrant and active community can help drive adoption and demand for the token.

6. Technical Considerations

Investors need to evaluate the technical aspects of the token to determine its potential value. A well-designed and secure blockchain technology is critical to the success of the token. Investors should also consider whether the technology is scalable and interoperable with other platforms. Code quality and audit reports are also important technical considerations.

7. Regulatory Considerations

Regulatory Considerations involve assessing any legal or regulatory risks associated with the token. Compliance with regulatory requirements is crucial to the token's long-term success. Investors need to be aware of any potential legal or regulatory challenges associated with the token and the project. They should also evaluate the project's legal and compliance framework to ensure that it is well-designed and meets regulatory standards.

By considering a wide range of factors, investors can gain a more complete picture of the token's potential value and viability. However, investors should always conduct their own research and seek professional advice before making any investment decisions.

100 Questions to ask

W hen looking at a Token and its tokenomics for your personal portfolio or as part of launching your own token, there are a few questions that you can ask to get a better understanding of the role of a token. This is a non-exhaustive list and should only work as a guideline. Many times, not all questions can be answered - though that is an important lesson in itself. We encourage you to add your own questions to this list and share your additions with us. We intentionally left space below each question for any notes and thoughts, making this a easy-to-use check-list that can help throughout your crypto journey.

General

1. Which tokens does the project use?

2. If there are several tokens, why?

3. What is the market cap of the token?

4. What is the circulating supply?

5. What is the maximum possible supply?

6. What is the Fully Diluted Valuation (FDV)?

7. Is the token's supply inflationary, stable, or deflationary?

8. Where can you buy the token?

9. Why is the token on these specific DEXes / CEXes?

10. How deep is the liquidity on these exchanges for the token?

11. How high is the token's volume on these exchanges?

12. Who are the main liquidity providers / market makers?

13. Are they in for the long term or incentivized via unsustainable token emissions?

14. Which parties do you put faith in when holding the token (ie chain, bridge, team, etc)?

15. Does the team benefit from the token appreciating?

16. Do users (not tokenholders) benefit from the token appreciating?

17. Can the project function without a token?

How the project launched its token

18. Why was this blockchain chosen to launch the token?

19. Is the chosen chain best for security, speed, or interoperability?

20. How old was the project when it launched the token?

21. Which token launch method was used?

22. How much did the project raise through its token launch?

23. At what Fully-Diluted Valuation (FDV) was the launch done?

24. How has the Market Cap / FDV changed since launch?

25. How does the chosen percentage of initial supply affect the emissions and token holder dilution in the future?

Supply

26. What factors affect the token's selling pressure?

27. How much will token supply grow in the future?

28. Who holds the token?

29. What % of supply do top 10 addresses control?

30. How about top 100 addresses?

31. When are VC and Team unlocks?

32. Have a large number of coins been lost or burned?

33. How much does the community hold?

34. How fair is the distribution?

35. What is the overall emissions schedule?

36. Who do emissions go to?

37. What is their behavior (do they sell off instantly or hold)?

38. Can you benefit from emissions by staking through LP?

39. Do emissions generate you profit, or just protect you against dilution?

40. Why are some released tokens not in circulating supply?

41. What will happen when locked (or staked) tokens are released?

42. Are there bulk unlocks in community lockup mechanisms?

Demand

43. What are the key drivers of demand for the token?

44. Are there other projects users can easily substitute to?

45. How did you find out about this project?

46. Will other people want this token in the future?

47. What is your expected return from holding the token?

48. Are there protocol revenues that get distributed to the token holders?

49. Does the project buy back and / or burn its own tokens?

50. Do tokens get destroyed or transferred when used to purchase a good / service from the protocol?

51. Does the project have a cult-like following?

52. How is the energy in their Discord?

53. How active is the project on Twitter?

54. How active is the community on Twitter?

55. How long have they been this active?

56. Will they be as active a month or a year from now?

57. Is there game theory driven incentive to hold the token?

58. Is there a token lockup mechanism?

59. Does it smell like a Ponzi scheme?

60. Is there a case for long-term demand?

Utility

61. What is the purpose of the token?

62. Are you supposed to hold it or use it for transactions / services?

63. What percentage of a project's cash flows are distributed to tokenholders?

64. Are cash flows dilutive or redistributive?

65. Do you plan to instantly sell or hold onto the earnings?

66. Is the token used for governance?

67. If yes, how concentrated are governance votes?

68. Will your vote make a difference?

69. What are the minimum token requirements to submit and escalate a governance proposal?

70. Can governance enable or affect profit distribution?

71. Are there bribes for governance voting that you can earn from?

72. Do the tokens secure the project?

73. Can the token be used as collateral to borrow liquidity?

Performance

74. Is the token correlated with the broader crypto market (ETH, BTC) or not?

75. Why would you want to hold the token instead of ETH or BTC?

76. How volatile is the token's price?

77. How has the token held up against USD or ETH since its inception?

78. Have emissions / staking earnings offset any of the losses?

79. What is the token's velocity?

80. What's the difference between current price and the ATH?

81. Has the token price been responsive to positive / negative news?

Bear Market & Other things

82. Do the tokenomics still make sense in the bear market?

83. How has the token been affected by the crash?

84. Do the tokenomics hold up during high volatility and other edge cases?

85. Does the token resemble a security (what are the chances of SEC knocking)?

86. Is there enough liquidity for you to exit quickly?

87. How about if everyone were to exit at the same time?

88. Are tokenomics affected by inflow / outflow of users?

89. Are there tranches to cover protocol losses incurred in black swan events?

90. Has the team adjusted tokenomics in the past?

91. Are there other projects with similar tokenomics and how are they doing?

92. Are there well-known holders?

93. Are they selling or accumulating?

94. Will the project remain relevant to see the next bull run?

95. Are the tokenomics of this project better than that of its direct competitors?

96. Has there been research into the tokenomics of this project?

97. Is the project behind the token doing well?

98. Are the tokenomics of the project overly complex and does that introduce more points of failure?

99. How available was the data to answer all of these questions?

100. Are you still sure you about the project?

Fourth Part

Conclusion

Closing Thoughts

A s we come to the end of this book on tokenomics, it is time for us to stop for a moment and reflect on our journey. We have explored the various aspects of evaluating crypto tokens from different perspectives, including token distribution, token utility, token economics, market dynamics, team and community, technical considerations, regulatory considerations, and tokenomics security. We have also discussed the challenges and opportunities in the crypto market and how tokenomics can help investors make informed decisions in this dynamic and rapidly evolving space.

I firmly hope that one of the main takeaways from this book is that tokenomics is a critical component in evaluating the potential risks and rewards of investing in a crypto token. Tokens don't always make sense. It is up to us to understand when and how they do. Understanding the tokenomics of a project can provide valuable insights into the token's potential value and viability, and help investors make more informed decisions. By evaluating a wide range of factors, such as the distribution model, token utility, market dynamics, technical considerations, and regulatory landscape, investors can gain a more complete picture of a token's potential value and the risks involved.

Despite the many opportunities that exist in the crypto token market, it is not without its challenges. The market is highly volatile and lacks sensible regulation, which can make investing in crypto tokens risky. Moreover, the complexity and technical nature of blockchain technology and smart contracts can make it difficult for investors to navigate the market. As such, conducting due diligence and seeking professional advice is crucial in mitigating risks and maximizing returns.

Looking ahead, we can expect to see continued growth and innovation in the crypto token market, with more use cases and applications being developed for blockchain technology. As the market matures, we may see increased regulation and standardization, which could help to reduce some of the risks associated with investing in crypto tokens. We may also see new tokenomics models being developed, such as decentralized finance (DeFi) and non-fungible tokens (NFTs), which could offer new investment opportunities and change the way we think about value in the digital world.

In conclusion, tokenomics is an essential tool for evaluating the potential risks and rewards of investing in crypto tokens. By considering a wide range of factors and conducting due diligence, investors can gain a more complete picture of a token's potential value and make more informed investment decisions. While the crypto token market is not without its challenges, the opportunities for growth and innovation are immense, and I am excited to see where the future of tokenomics takes us.

Acknowledgments

T his book wouldn't have been possible without the help and input of many people. A big thank you belongs to my former boss at Binance Research, who taught me more than I thought was possible. He managed to be a great leader and a huge inspiration and source of knowledge. A big thank you also belongs to my former colleagues Shivam and Jie Xuan, as well as L, B, D, K, and J (you know who you are).

I also want to thank Bill for the insightful discussions we had, as well as Ilmira, for her organizational work on making this book possible.

Thank you to everyone who crossed my path and taught me an important lesson.

Tokenomics

Stefan Piech

Tokenomics

Made in the USA
Las Vegas, NV
14 December 2023

82831431R00246